P9-ARH-846

A WHO HQ GRAPHIC NOVEL

Who Was the Girl Warrior of France?

JOAN OF ARC

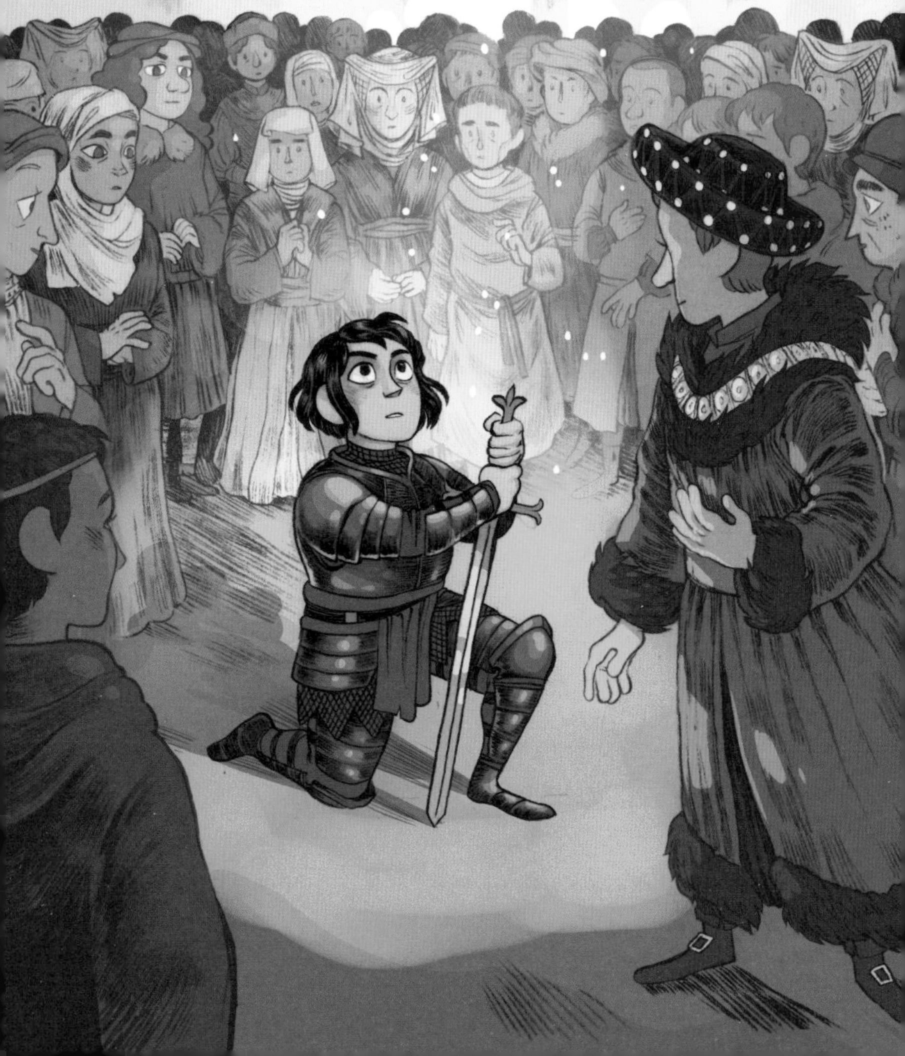

For Kiran, Laiken, Aleah, and all the
little historians out there—SWS

For Amanda—MCF

PENGUIN WORKSHOP
An Imprint of Penguin Random House LLC, New York

Penguin supports copyright. Copyright fuels creativity, encourages diverse voices,
promotes free speech, and creates a vibrant culture. Thank you for buying an authorized
edition of this book and for complying with copyright laws by not reproducing, scanning,
or distributing any part of it in any form without permission. You are supporting writers
and allowing Penguin to continue to publish books for every reader.

The publisher does not have any control over and does not assume any responsibility for author
or third-party websites or their content.

Copyright © 2021 by Penguin Random House LLC. All rights reserved.
Published by Penguin Workshop, an imprint of Penguin Random House LLC, New York.
PENGUIN and PENGUIN WORKSHOP are trademarks of Penguin Books Ltd.
WHO HQ & Design is a registered trademark of Penguin Random House LLC.
Manufactured in China.

Visit us online at www.penguinrandomhouse.com.

Library of Congress Cataloging-in-Publication Data is available upon request.

ISBN 9780593224403 (pbk)   10 9 8 7 6 5 4 3 2 1 HH
ISBN 9780593224410 (hc)   10 9 8 7 6 5 4 3 2 1 HH

Lettering by Comicraft
Book design by Jay Emmanuel

This is a work of nonfiction. All of the events that unfold in the narrative
are rooted in historical fact. Some dialogue and characters have been fictionalized
in order to illustrate or teach a historical point.

For more information about your favorite historical figures, places, and events,
please visit www.whohq.com.

A WHO HQ GRAPHIC NOVEL

Who Was the Girl Warrior of France?

JOAN OF ARC

by Sarah Winifred Searle
illustrated by Maria Capelle Frantz

Penguin Workshop

Introduction

Joan of Arc is the English name for a girl from France whose first name was "Jeanne" and whose last name was "d'Arc"—Jeanne d'Arc in French.

Jeanne d'Arc took a deep breath of cold January air while she finished helping her father, Jacques, and three brothers with the early morning farm chores one last time. Jeanne's sister and her mother, Isabelle, greeted them with wooden bowls of hot porridge as they hurried back inside to sit around the fireplace. Jeanne took a minute from her breakfast to appreciate how cozy this house felt when filled with her family and their voices. She was going to miss this warmth.

Jeanne was nervous—today, she was leaving home in Domrémy for the town of Vaucouleurs. She was only sixteen years old, but God's angels had been visiting her through visions since she was thirteen. The angels—Saint Michael, Saint Catherine, and Saint Margaret—spoke to her through the shifting light of her church's candles, the whistle of the wind, and the ache in her heart when she thought about the war that was happening around her. They revealed God's mission for her: Heaven chose Jeanne, also known as Joan of Arc, to end the Hundred Years' War and lead France to freedom.

The mission felt huge. The war had been raging on and off

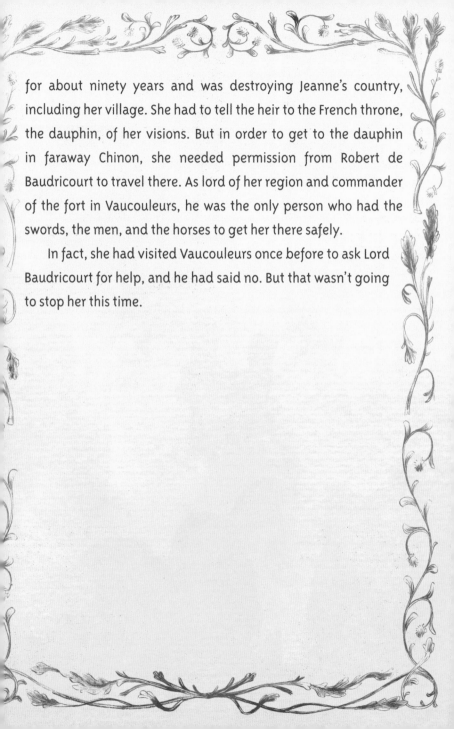

for about ninety years and was destroying Jeanne's country, including her village. She had to tell the heir to the French throne, the dauphin, of her visions. But in order to get to the dauphin in faraway Chinon, she needed permission from Robert de Baudricourt to travel there. As lord of her region and commander of the fort in Vaucouleurs, he was the only person who had the swords, the men, and the horses to get her there safely.

In fact, she had visited Vaucouleurs once before to ask Lord Baudricourt for help, and he had said no. But that wasn't going to stop her this time.

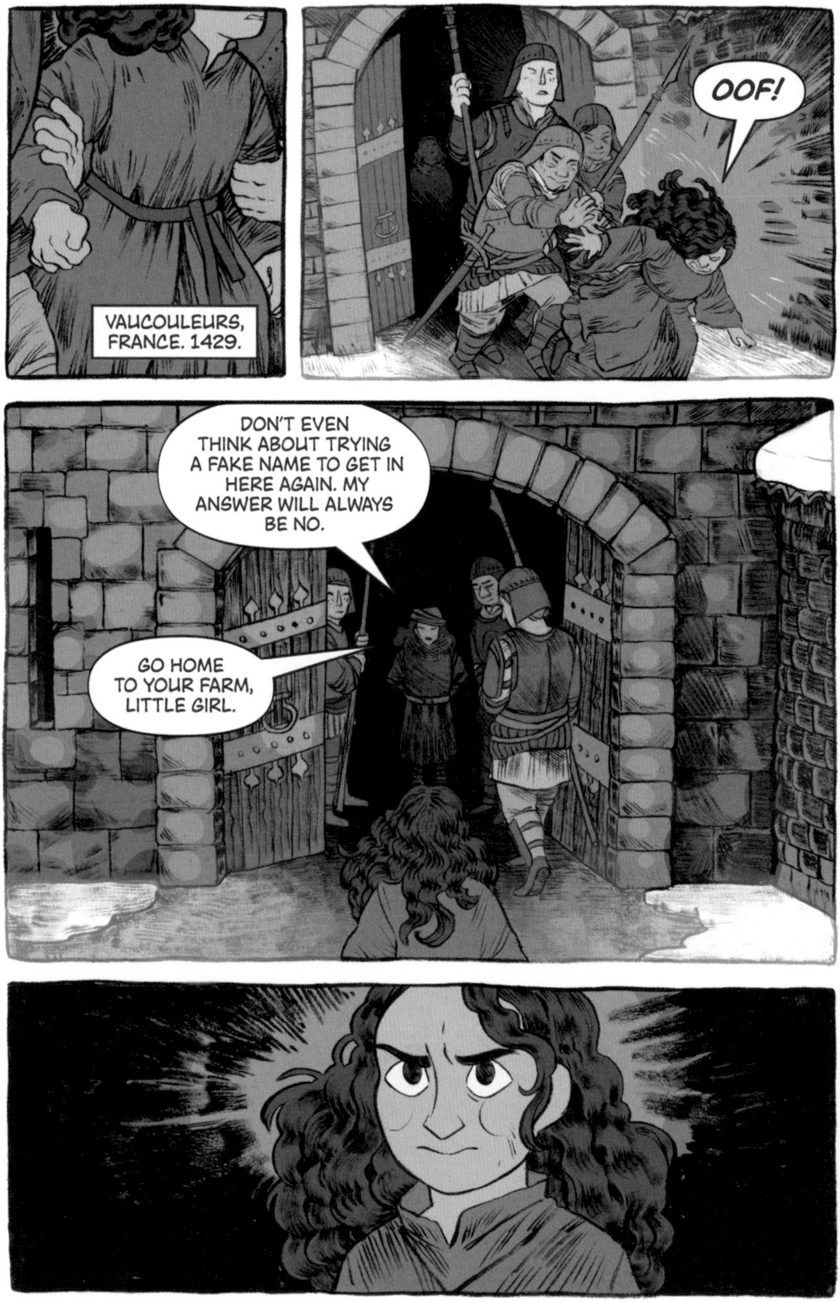
VAUCOULEURS, FRANCE. 1429.
OOF!
DON'T EVEN THINK ABOUT TRYING A FAKE NAME TO GET IN HERE AGAIN. MY ANSWER WILL ALWAYS BE NO.
GO HOME TO YOUR FARM, LITTLE GIRL.

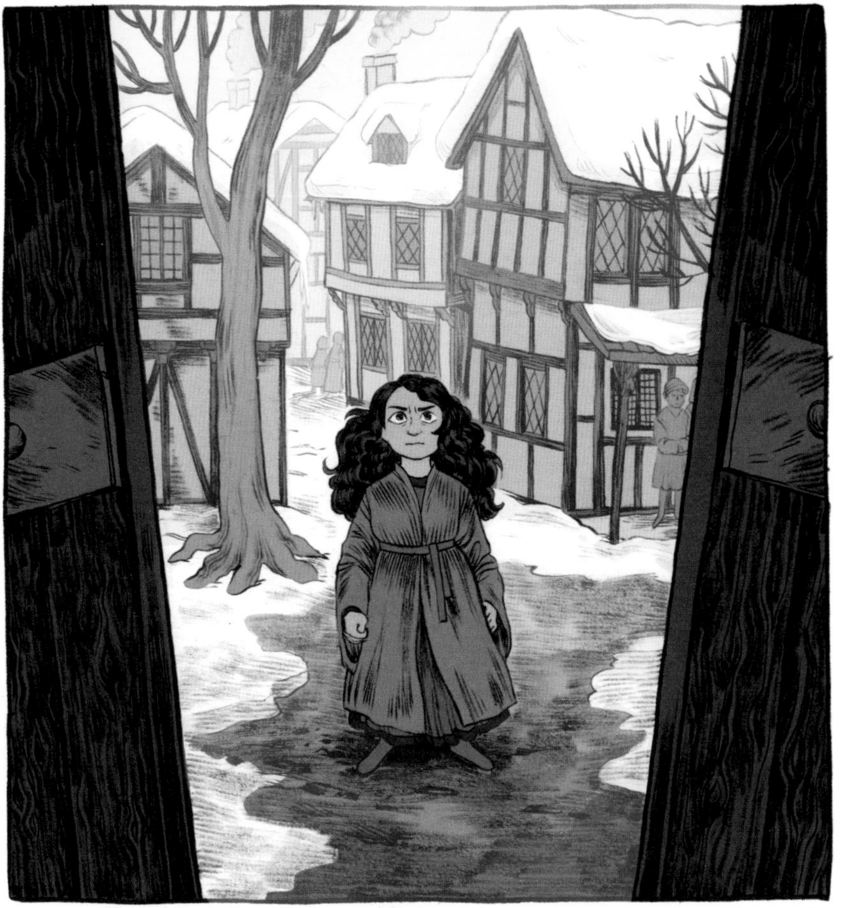

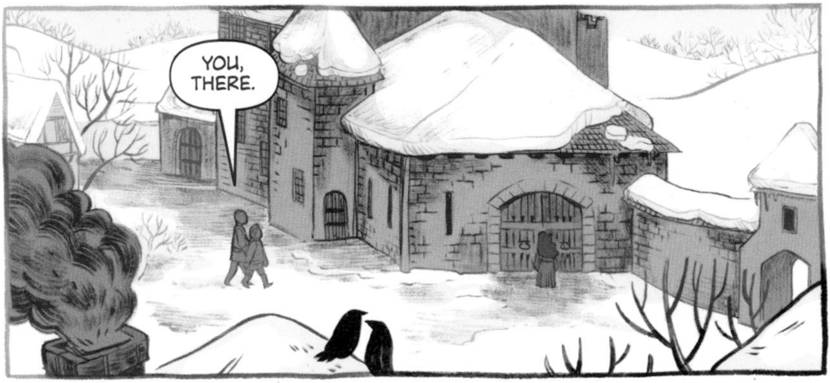
YOU, THERE.

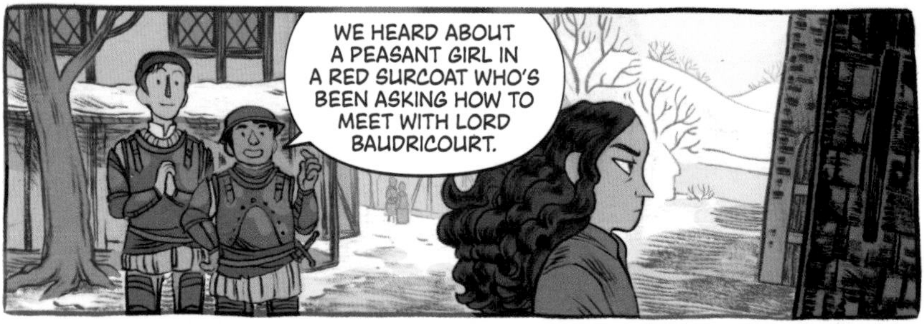
WE HEARD ABOUT A PEASANT GIRL IN A RED SURCOAT WHO'S BEEN ASKING HOW TO MEET WITH LORD BAUDRICOURT.

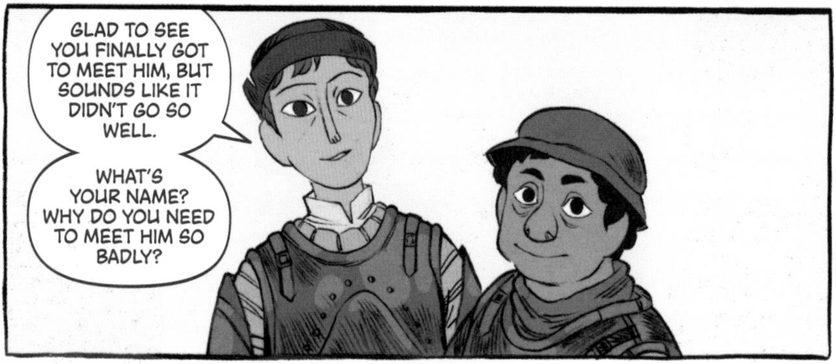
GLAD TO SEE YOU FINALLY GOT TO MEET HIM, BUT SOUNDS LIKE IT DIDN'T GO SO WELL.
WHAT'S YOUR NAME? WHY DO YOU NEED TO MEET HIM SO BADLY?

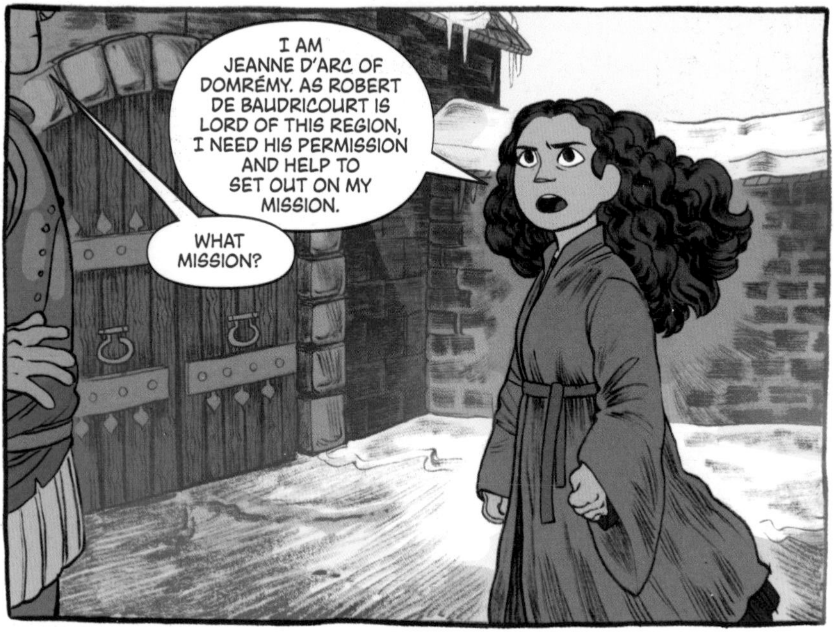
I AM JEANNE D'ARC OF DOMRÉMY. AS ROBERT DE BAUDRICOURT IS LORD OF THIS REGION, I NEED HIS PERMISSION AND HELP TO SET OUT ON MY MISSION.
WHAT MISSION?

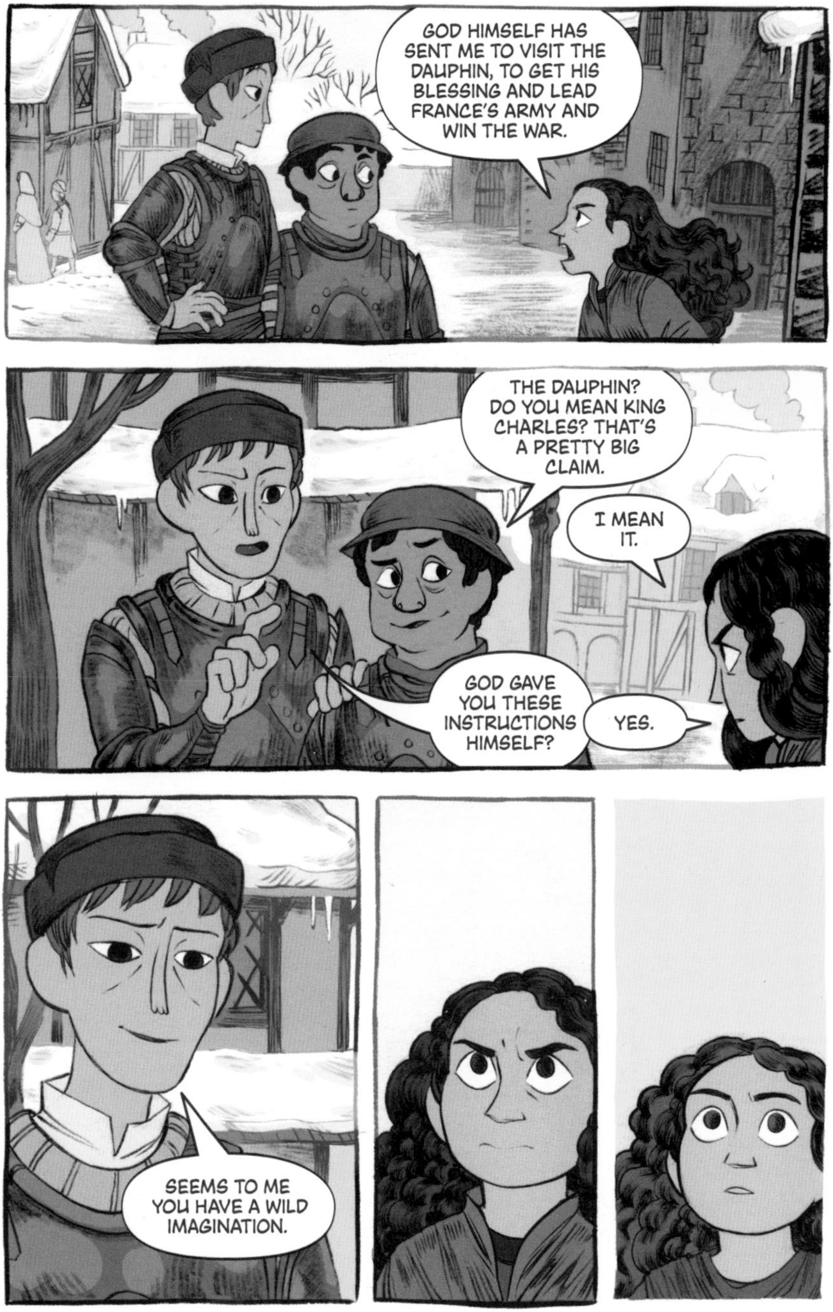
GOD HIMSELF HAS SENT ME TO VISIT THE DAUPHIN, TO GET HIS BLESSING AND LEAD FRANCE'S ARMY AND WIN THE WAR.
THE DAUPHIN? DO YOU MEAN KING CHARLES? THAT'S A PRETTY BIG CLAIM.
I MEAN IT.
GOD GAVE YOU THESE INSTRUCTIONS HIMSELF?
YES.
SEEMS TO ME YOU HAVE A WILD IMAGINATION.

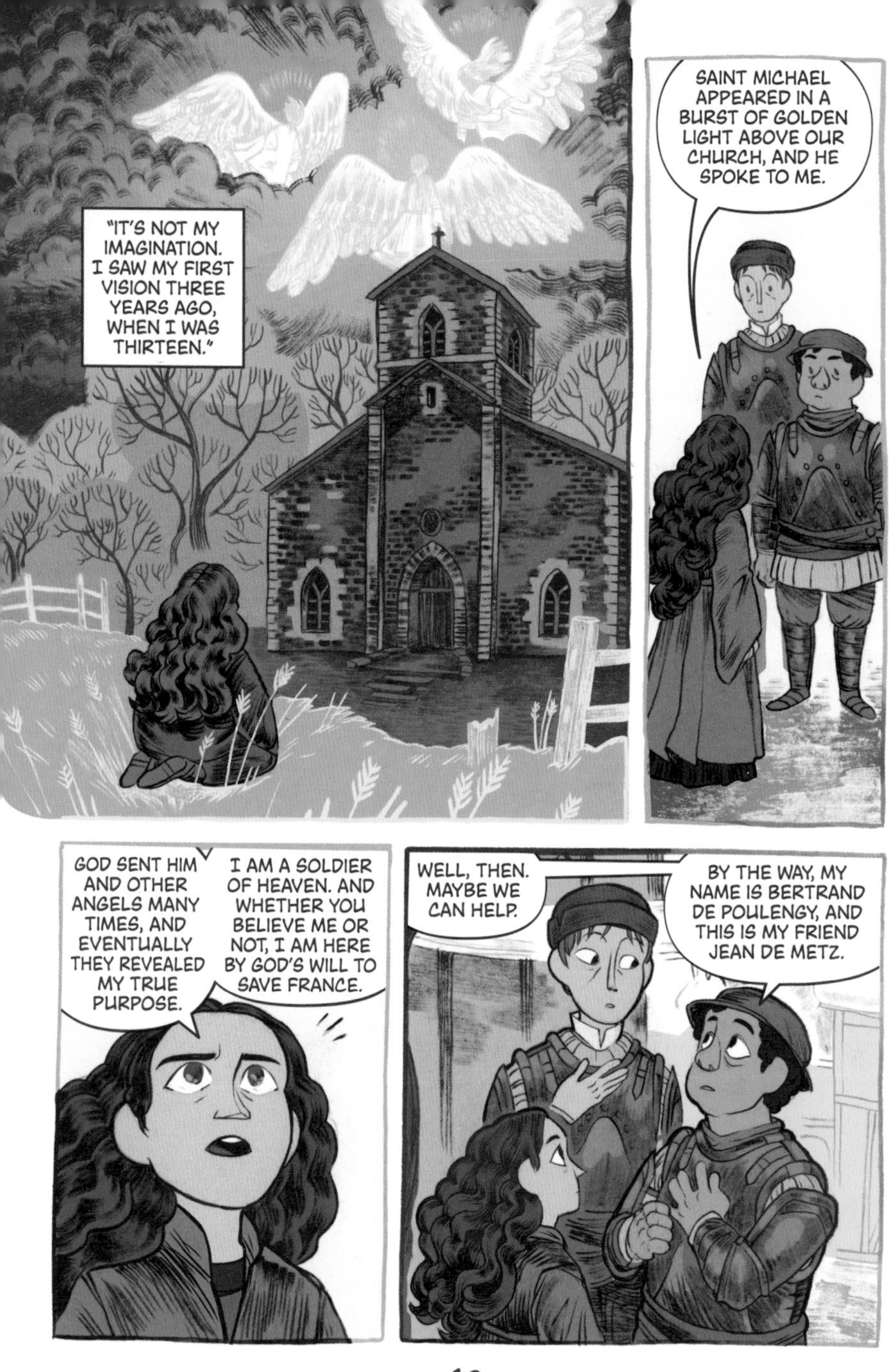
"IT'S NOT MY IMAGINATION. I SAW MY FIRST VISION THREE YEARS AGO, WHEN I WAS THIRTEEN."
SAINT MICHAEL APPEARED IN A BURST OF GOLDEN LIGHT ABOVE OUR CHURCH, AND HE SPOKE TO ME.
GOD SENT HIM AND OTHER ANGELS MANY TIMES, AND EVENTUALLY THEY REVEALED MY TRUE PURPOSE.
I AM A SOLDIER OF HEAVEN. AND WHETHER YOU BELIEVE ME OR NOT, I AM HERE BY GOD'S WILL TO SAVE FRANCE.
WELL, THEN. MAYBE WE CAN HELP.
BY THE WAY, MY NAME IS BERTRAND DE POULENGY, AND THIS IS MY FRIEND JEAN DE METZ.

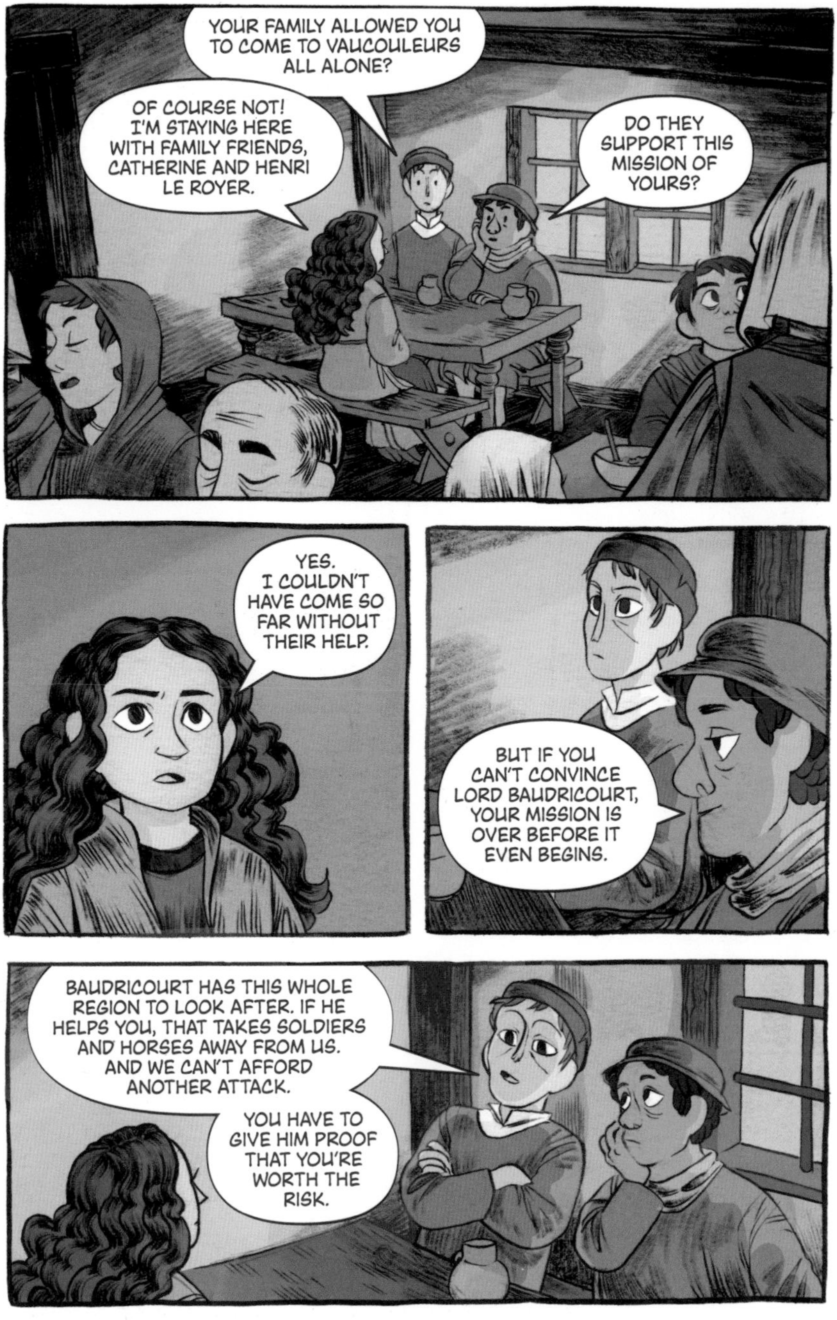
YOUR FAMILY ALLOWED YOU TO COME TO VAUCOULEURS ALL ALONE?
OF COURSE NOT! I'M STAYING HERE WITH FAMILY FRIENDS, CATHERINE AND HENRI LE ROYER.
DO THEY SUPPORT THIS MISSION OF YOURS?
YES. I COULDN'T HAVE COME SO FAR WITHOUT THEIR HELP.
BUT IF YOU CAN'T CONVINCE LORD BAUDRICOURT, YOUR MISSION IS OVER BEFORE IT EVEN BEGINS.
BAUDRICOURT HAS THIS WHOLE REGION TO LOOK AFTER. IF HE HELPS YOU, THAT TAKES SOLDIERS AND HORSES AWAY FROM US. AND WE CAN'T AFFORD ANOTHER ATTACK.
YOU HAVE TO GIVE HIM PROOF THAT YOU'RE WORTH THE RISK.

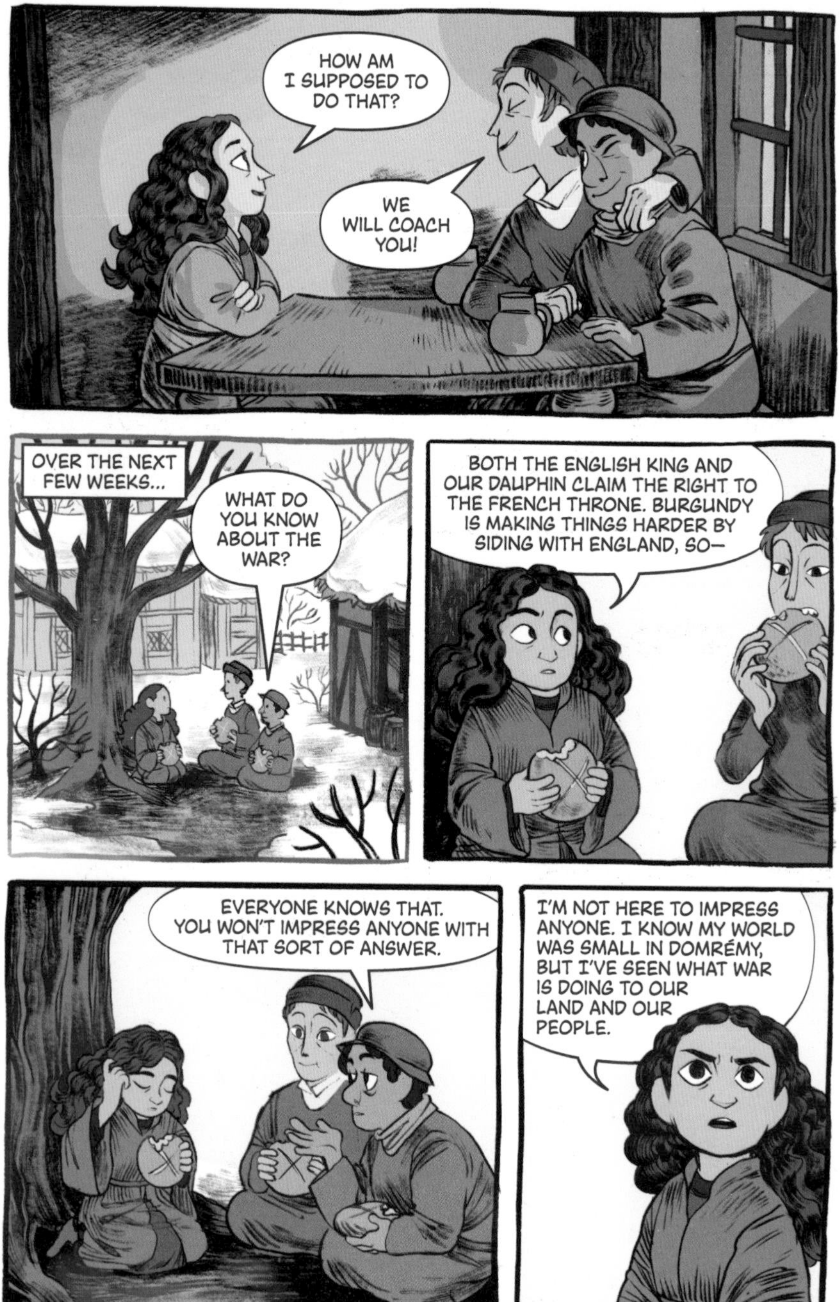
HOW AM I SUPPOSED TO DO THAT?
WE WILL COACH YOU!
OVER THE NEXT FEW WEEKS...
WHAT DO YOU KNOW ABOUT THE WAR?
BOTH THE ENGLISH KING AND OUR DAUPHIN CLAIM THE RIGHT TO THE FRENCH THRONE. BURGUNDY IS MAKING THINGS HARDER BY SIDING WITH ENGLAND, SO—
EVERYONE KNOWS THAT. YOU WON'T IMPRESS ANYONE WITH THAT SORT OF ANSWER.
I'M NOT HERE TO IMPRESS ANYONE. I KNOW MY WORLD WAS SMALL IN DOMRÉMY, BUT I'VE SEEN WHAT WAR IS DOING TO OUR LAND AND OUR PEOPLE.

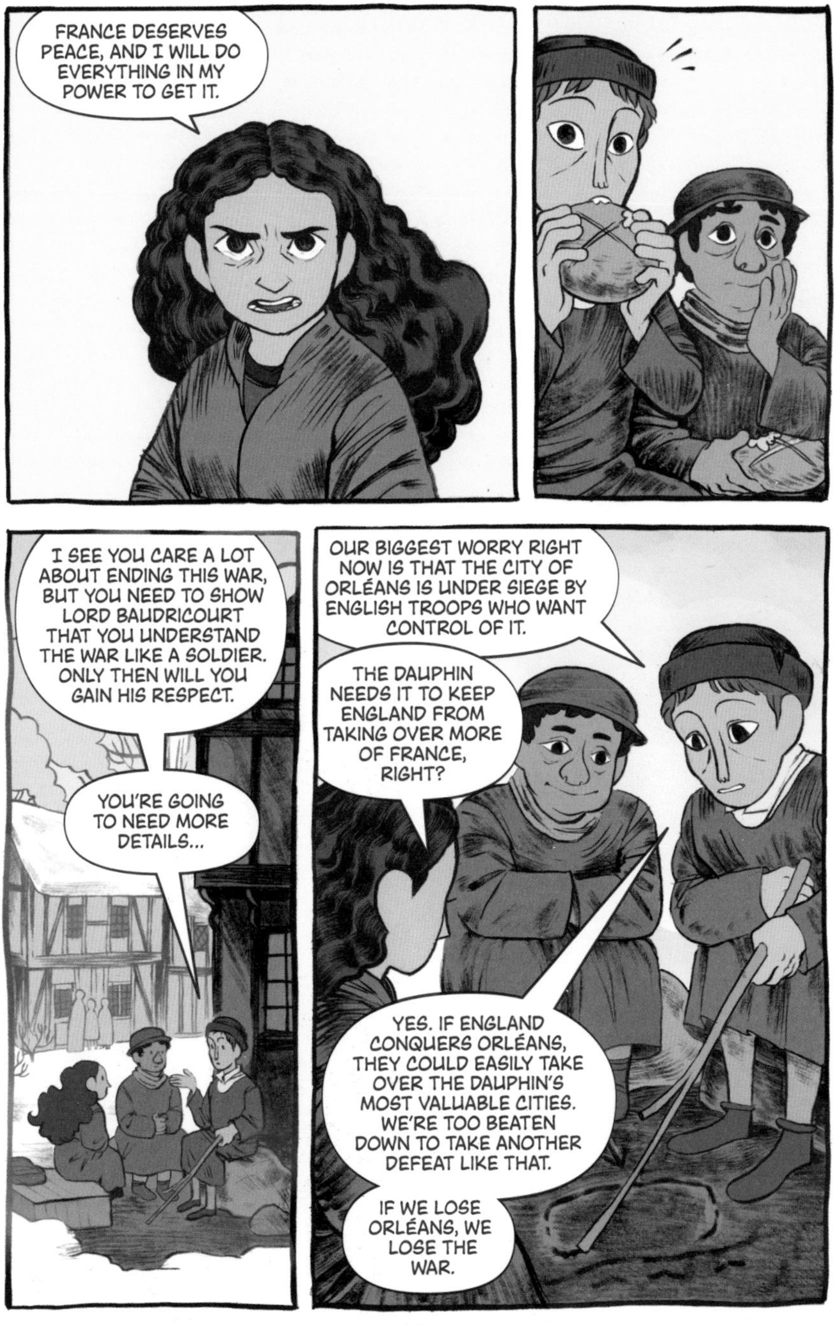
FRANCE DESERVES PEACE, AND I WILL DO EVERYTHING IN MY POWER TO GET IT.
I SEE YOU CARE A LOT ABOUT ENDING THIS WAR, BUT YOU NEED TO SHOW LORD BAUDRICOURT THAT YOU UNDERSTAND THE WAR LIKE A SOLDIER. ONLY THEN WILL YOU GAIN HIS RESPECT.
YOU'RE GOING TO NEED MORE DETAILS...
OUR BIGGEST WORRY RIGHT NOW IS THAT THE CITY OF ORLÉANS IS UNDER SIEGE BY ENGLISH TROOPS WHO WANT CONTROL OF IT.
THE DAUPHIN NEEDS IT TO KEEP ENGLAND FROM TAKING OVER MORE OF FRANCE, RIGHT?
YES. IF ENGLAND CONQUERS ORLÉANS, THEY COULD EASILY TAKE OVER THE DAUPHIN'S MOST VALUABLE CITIES. WE'RE TOO BEATEN DOWN TO TAKE ANOTHER DEFEAT LIKE THAT.
IF WE LOSE ORLÉANS, WE LOSE THE WAR.

The Hundred Years' War

In 1328, King Charles IV of France died. With no sons to inherit the throne, two different royal families soon claimed the right to rule France. King Edward III of England thought he should be king because he was Charles IV's nephew. But France had other plans—they crowned Charles IV's French cousin, King Philip VI, as the rightful heir. To make matters more complicated, Burgundy, France's neighbor to the west, sided with England in the fight.

This began a war that lasted on and off from 1337 to 1453. English and Burgundian soldiers often raided French villages by attacking and killing innocent people and stealing their food and valuables. France's citizens couldn't feel safe with this war that seemed like it would never end.

Over the course of the Hundred Years' War, somewhere between two and three million people died.

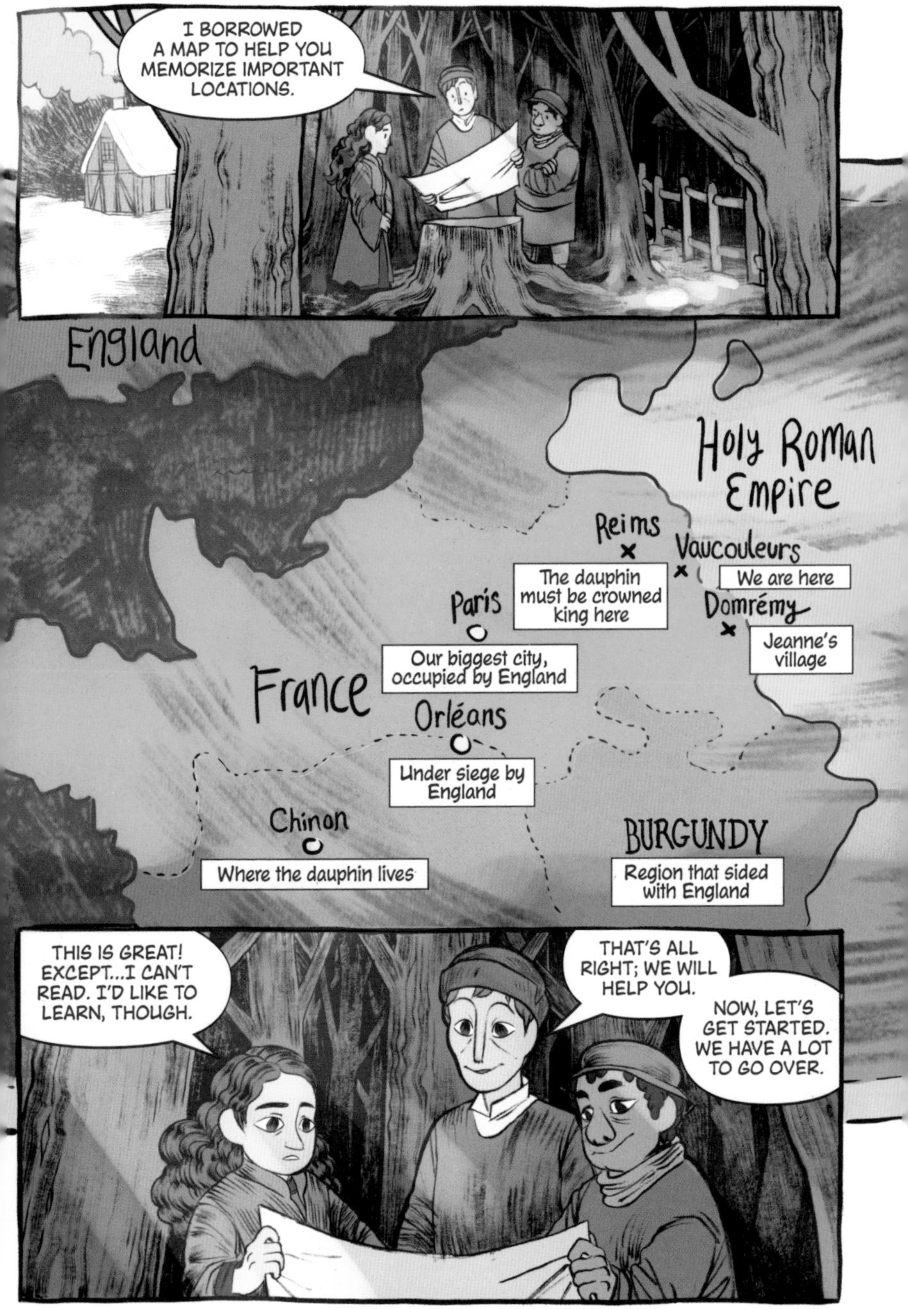
I BORROWED A MAP TO HELP YOU MEMORIZE IMPORTANT LOCATIONS.
England
Holy Roman Empire
Reims
The dauphin must be crowned king here
Vaucouleurs
We are here
Domrémy
Jeanne's village
Paris
Our biggest city, occupied by England
France
Orléans
Under siege by England
Chinon
Where the dauphin lives
BURGUNDY
Region that sided with England
THIS IS GREAT! EXCEPT...I CAN'T READ. I'D LIKE TO LEARN, THOUGH.
THAT'S ALL RIGHT; WE WILL HELP YOU.
NOW, LET'S GET STARTED. WE HAVE A LOT TO GO OVER.

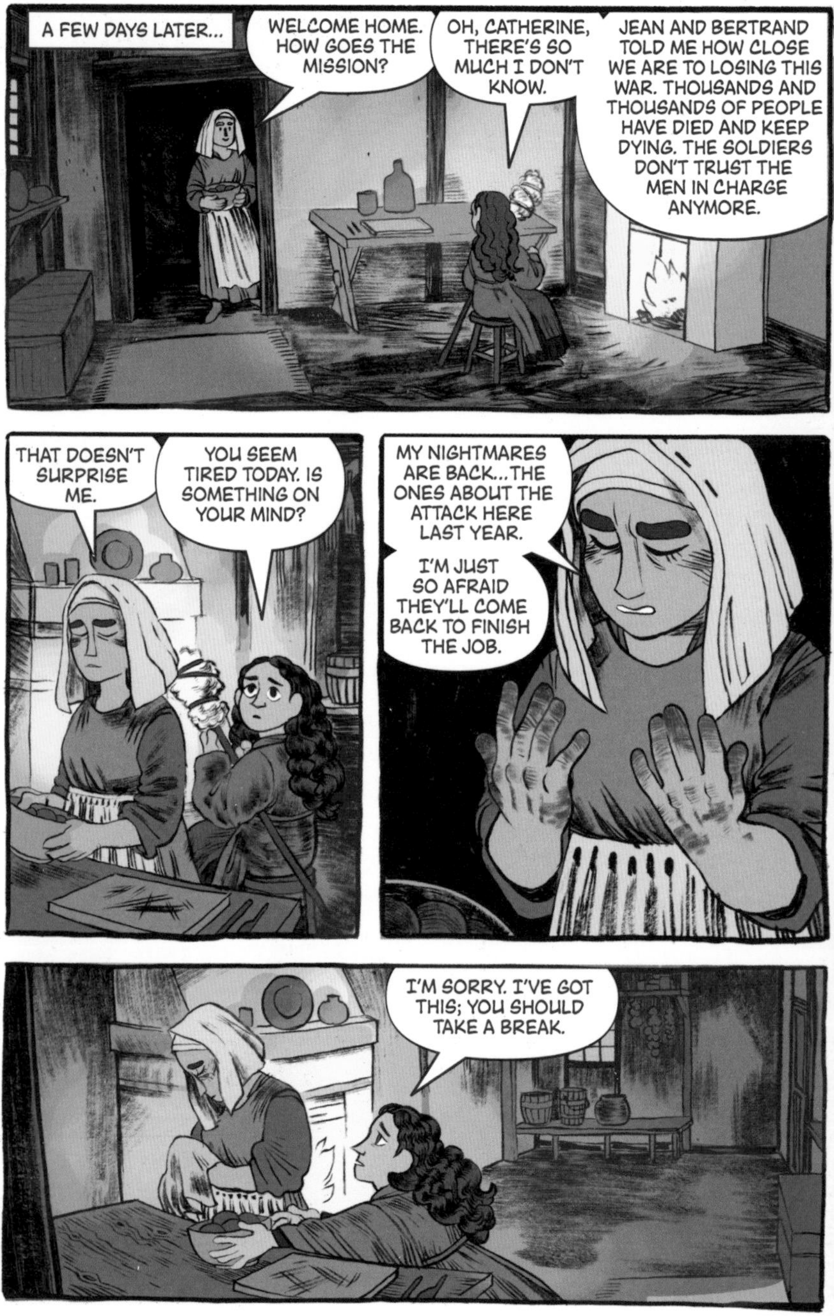
A FEW DAYS LATER...
WELCOME HOME. HOW GOES THE MISSION?
OH, CATHERINE, THERE'S SO MUCH I DON'T KNOW.
JEAN AND BERTRAND TOLD ME HOW CLOSE WE ARE TO LOSING THIS WAR. THOUSANDS AND THOUSANDS OF PEOPLE HAVE DIED AND KEEP DYING. THE SOLDIERS DON'T TRUST THE MEN IN CHARGE ANYMORE.
THAT DOESN'T SURPRISE ME.
YOU SEEM TIRED TODAY. IS SOMETHING ON YOUR MIND?
MY NIGHTMARES ARE BACK...THE ONES ABOUT THE ATTACK HERE LAST YEAR.
I'M JUST SO AFRAID THEY'LL COME BACK TO FINISH THE JOB.
I'M SORRY. I'VE GOT THIS; YOU SHOULD TAKE A BREAK.

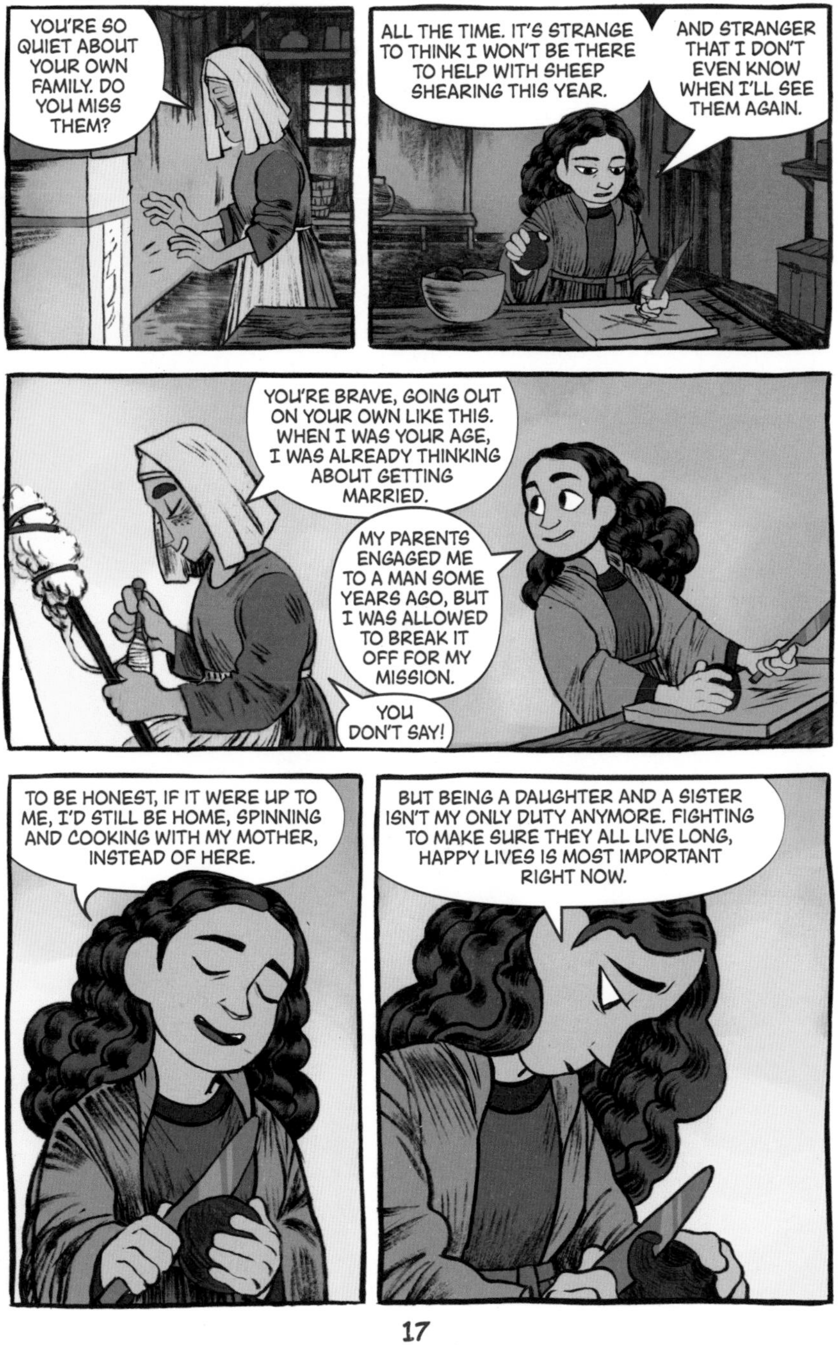
YOU'RE SO QUIET ABOUT YOUR OWN FAMILY. DO YOU MISS THEM?
ALL THE TIME. IT'S STRANGE TO THINK I WON'T BE THERE TO HELP WITH SHEEP SHEARING THIS YEAR.
AND STRANGER THAT I DON'T EVEN KNOW WHEN I'LL SEE THEM AGAIN.
YOU'RE BRAVE, GOING OUT ON YOUR OWN LIKE THIS. WHEN I WAS YOUR AGE, I WAS ALREADY THINKING ABOUT GETTING MARRIED.
MY PARENTS ENGAGED ME TO A MAN SOME YEARS AGO, BUT I WAS ALLOWED TO BREAK IT OFF FOR MY MISSION.
YOU DON'T SAY!
TO BE HONEST, IF IT WERE UP TO ME, I'D STILL BE HOME, SPINNING AND COOKING WITH MY MOTHER, INSTEAD OF HERE.
BUT BEING A DAUGHTER AND A SISTER ISN'T MY ONLY DUTY ANYMORE. FIGHTING TO MAKE SURE THEY ALL LIVE LONG, HAPPY LIVES IS MOST IMPORTANT RIGHT NOW.

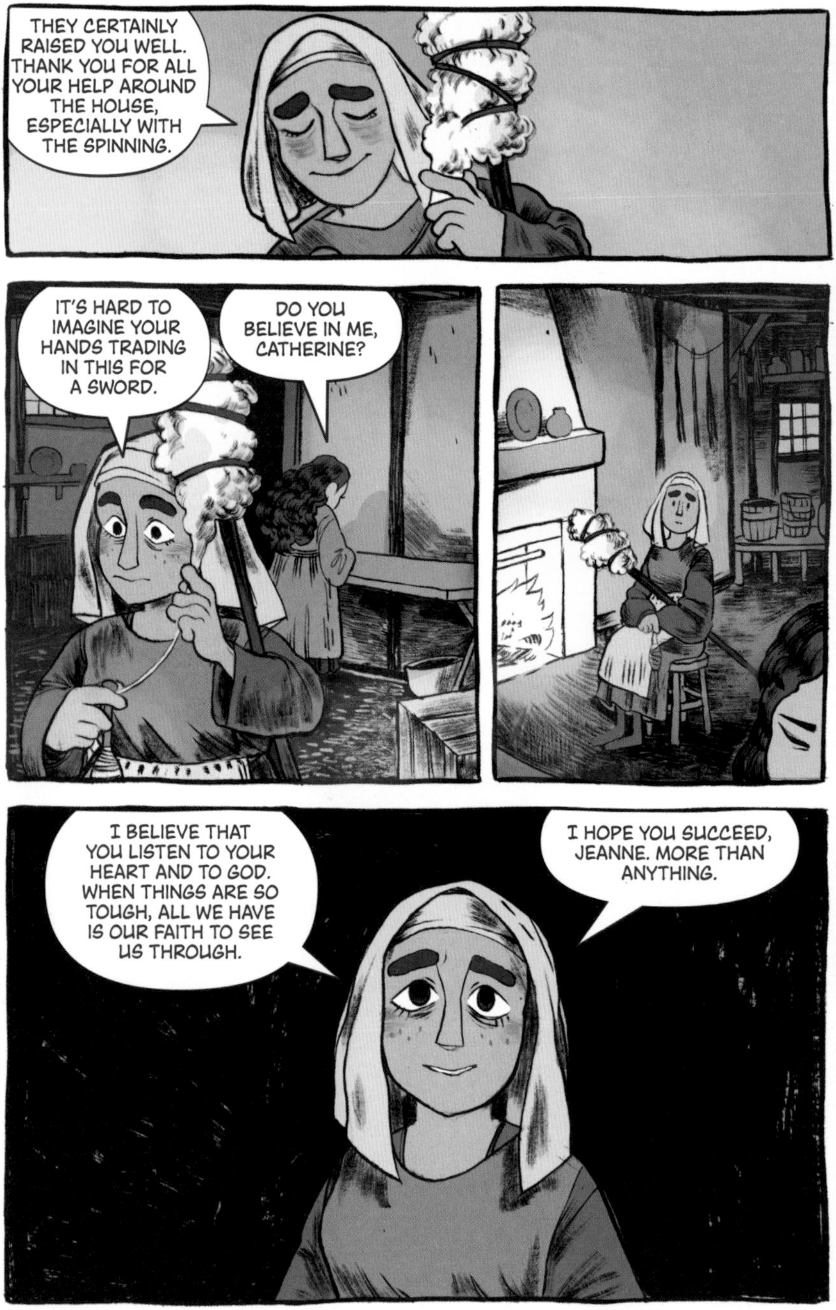

THEY CERTAINLY RAISED YOU WELL. THANK YOU FOR ALL YOUR HELP AROUND THE HOUSE, ESPECIALLY WITH THE SPINNING.
IT'S HARD TO IMAGINE YOUR HANDS TRADING IN THIS FOR A SWORD.
DO YOU BELIEVE IN ME, CATHERINE?
I BELIEVE THAT YOU LISTEN TO YOUR HEART AND TO GOD. WHEN THINGS ARE SO TOUGH, ALL WE HAVE IS OUR FAITH TO SEE US THROUGH.
I HOPE YOU SUCCEED, JEANNE. MORE THAN ANYTHING.

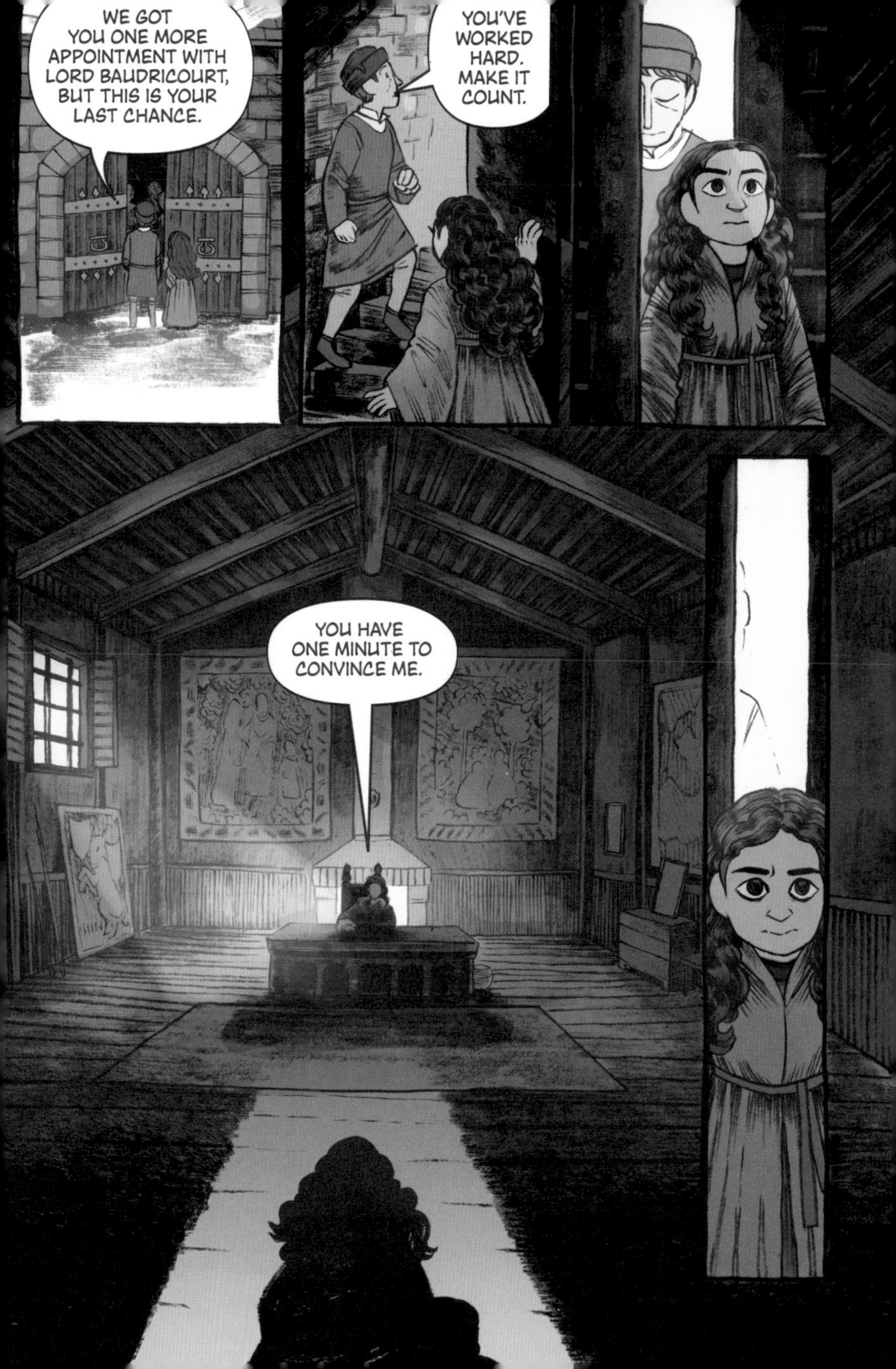
WE GOT YOU ONE MORE APPOINTMENT WITH LORD BAUDRICOURT, BUT THIS IS YOUR LAST CHANCE.
YOU'VE WORKED HARD. MAKE IT COUNT.
YOU HAVE ONE MINUTE TO CONVINCE ME.

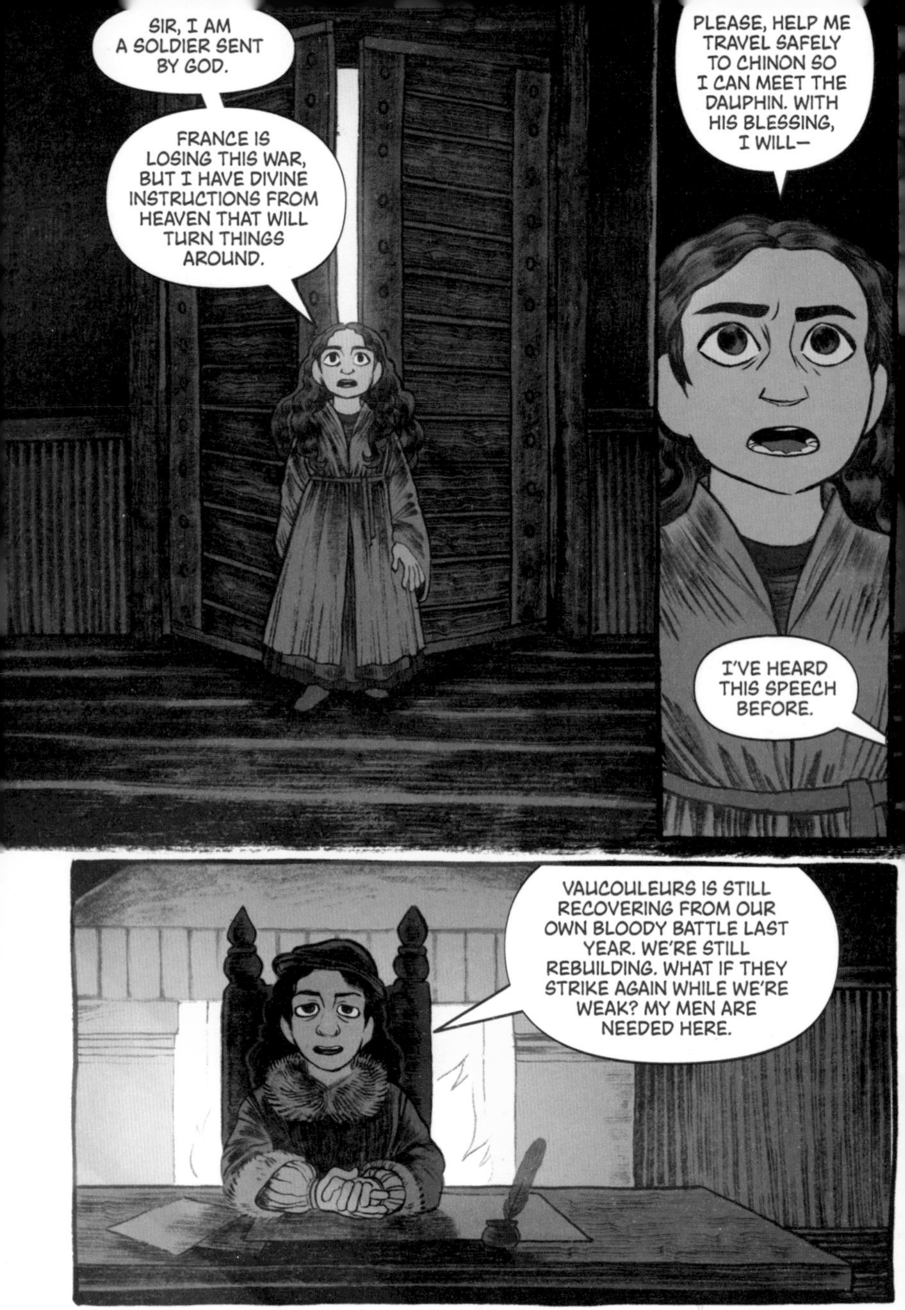
SIR, I AM A SOLDIER SENT BY GOD.
FRANCE IS LOSING THIS WAR, BUT I HAVE DIVINE INSTRUCTIONS FROM HEAVEN THAT WILL TURN THINGS AROUND.
PLEASE, HELP ME TRAVEL SAFELY TO CHINON SO I CAN MEET THE DAUPHIN. WITH HIS BLESSING, I WILL—
I'VE HEARD THIS SPEECH BEFORE.
VAUCOULEURS IS STILL RECOVERING FROM OUR OWN BLOODY BATTLE LAST YEAR. WE'RE STILL REBUILDING. WHAT IF THEY STRIKE AGAIN WHILE WE'RE WEAK? MY MEN ARE NEEDED HERE.

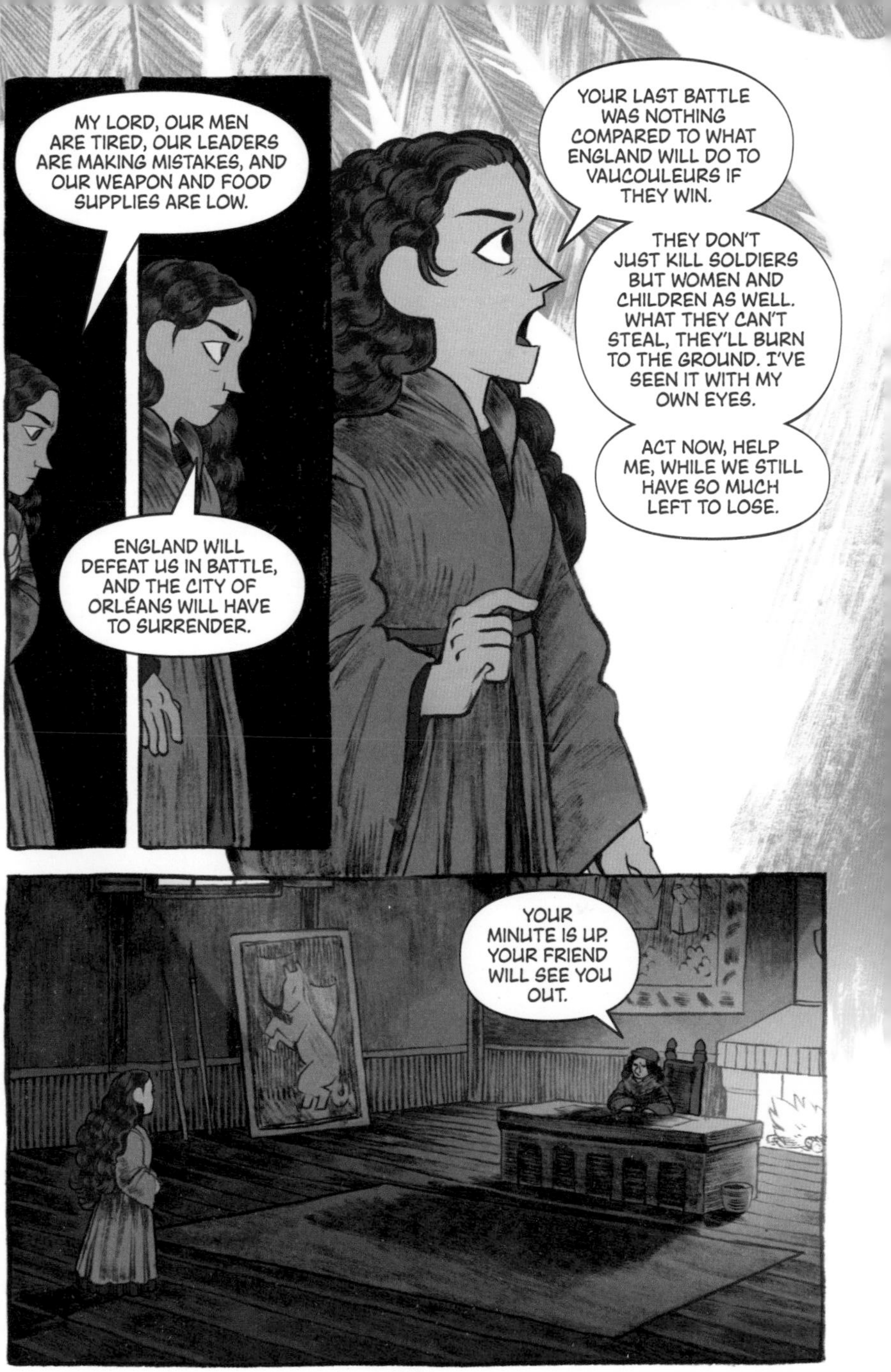
MY LORD, OUR MEN ARE TIRED, OUR LEADERS ARE MAKING MISTAKES, AND OUR WEAPON AND FOOD SUPPLIES ARE LOW.
ENGLAND WILL DEFEAT US IN BATTLE, AND THE CITY OF ORLÉANS WILL HAVE TO SURRENDER.
YOUR LAST BATTLE WAS NOTHING COMPARED TO WHAT ENGLAND WILL DO TO VAUCOULEURS IF THEY WIN.
THEY DON'T JUST KILL SOLDIERS BUT WOMEN AND CHILDREN AS WELL. WHAT THEY CAN'T STEAL, THEY'LL BURN TO THE GROUND. I'VE SEEN IT WITH MY OWN EYES.
ACT NOW, HELP ME, WHILE WE STILL HAVE SO MUCH LEFT TO LOSE.
YOUR MINUTE IS UP. YOUR FRIEND WILL SEE YOU OUT.

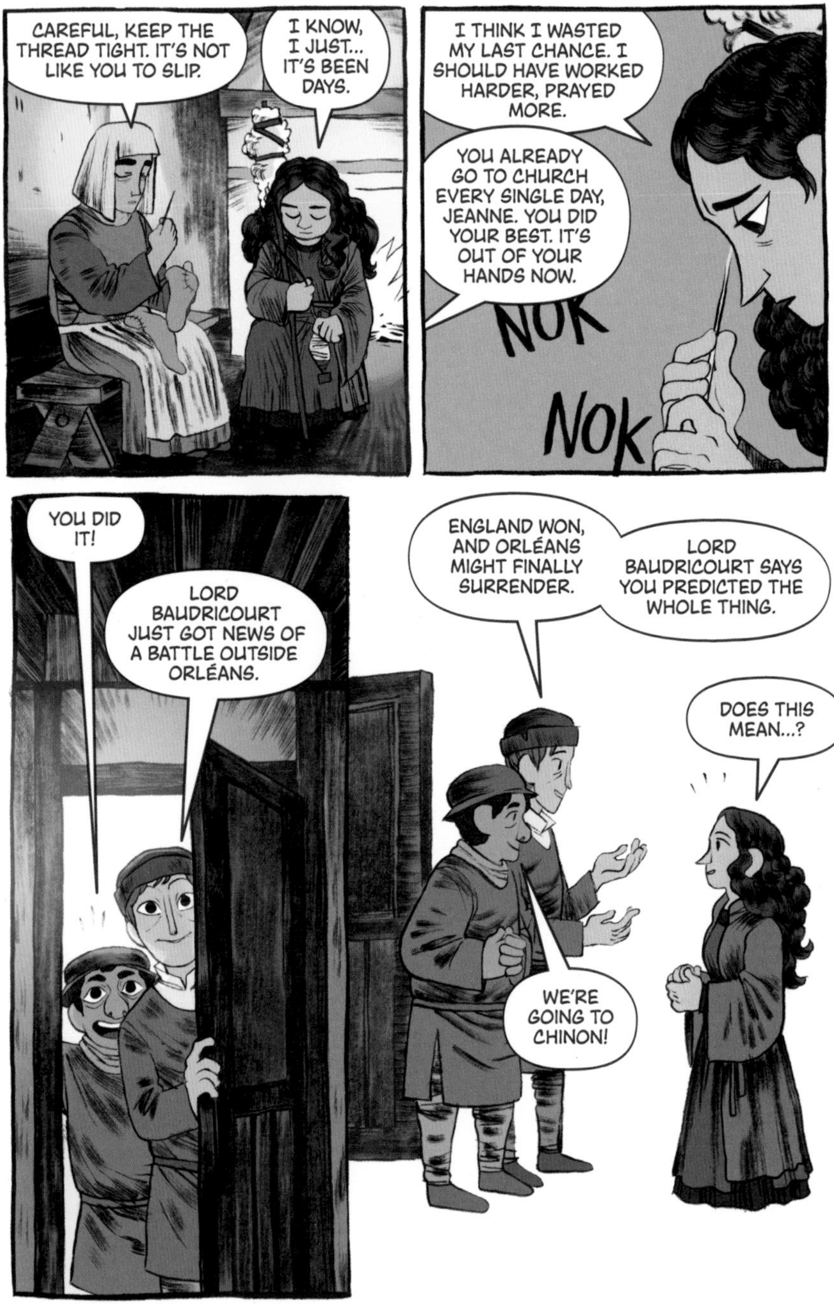
CAREFUL, KEEP THE THREAD TIGHT. IT'S NOT LIKE YOU TO SLIP.
I KNOW, I JUST... IT'S BEEN DAYS.
I THINK I WASTED MY LAST CHANCE. I SHOULD HAVE WORKED HARDER, PRAYED MORE.
YOU ALREADY GO TO CHURCH EVERY SINGLE DAY, JEANNE. YOU DID YOUR BEST. IT'S OUT OF YOUR HANDS NOW.
NOK
NOK
YOU DID IT!
LORD BAUDRICOURT JUST GOT NEWS OF A BATTLE OUTSIDE ORLÉANS.
ENGLAND WON, AND ORLÉANS MIGHT FINALLY SURRENDER.
LORD BAUDRICOURT SAYS YOU PREDICTED THE WHOLE THING.
WE'RE GOING TO CHINON!
DOES THIS MEAN...?

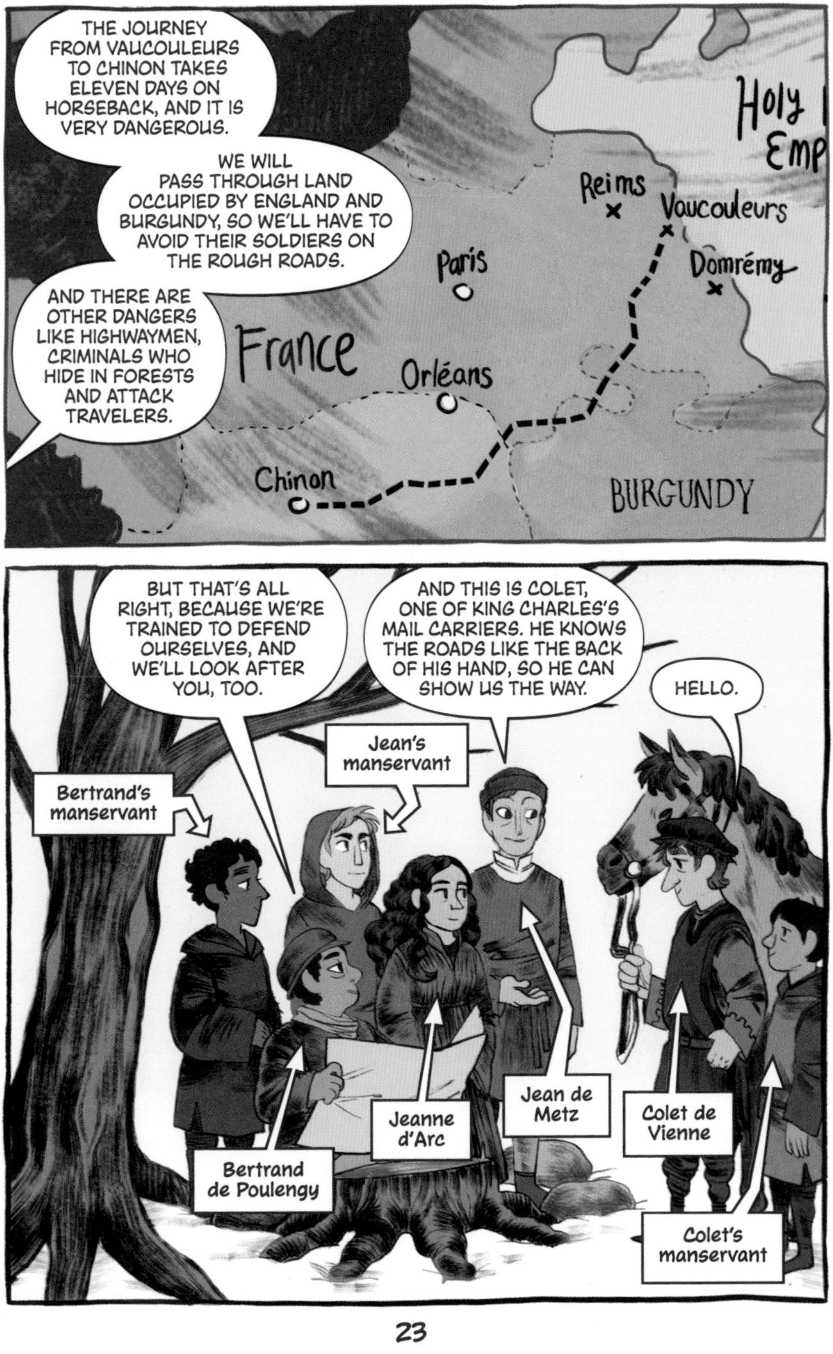
THE JOURNEY FROM VAUCOULEURS TO CHINON TAKES ELEVEN DAYS ON HORSEBACK, AND IT IS VERY DANGEROUS.
WE WILL PASS THROUGH LAND OCCUPIED BY ENGLAND AND BURGUNDY, SO WE'LL HAVE TO AVOID THEIR SOLDIERS ON THE ROUGH ROADS.
AND THERE ARE OTHER DANGERS LIKE HIGHWAYMEN, CRIMINALS WHO HIDE IN FORESTS AND ATTACK TRAVELERS.
Reims
Vaucouleurs
Paris
Domrémy
France
Orléans
Chinon
BURGUNDY
BUT THAT'S ALL RIGHT, BECAUSE WE'RE TRAINED TO DEFEND OURSELVES, AND WE'LL LOOK AFTER YOU, TOO.
AND THIS IS COLET, ONE OF KING CHARLES'S MAIL CARRIERS. HE KNOWS THE ROADS LIKE THE BACK OF HIS HAND, SO HE CAN SHOW US THE WAY.
HELLO.
Jean's manservant
Bertrand's manservant
Jean de Metz
Jeanne d'Arc
Bertrand de Poulengy
Colet de Vienne
Colet's manservant

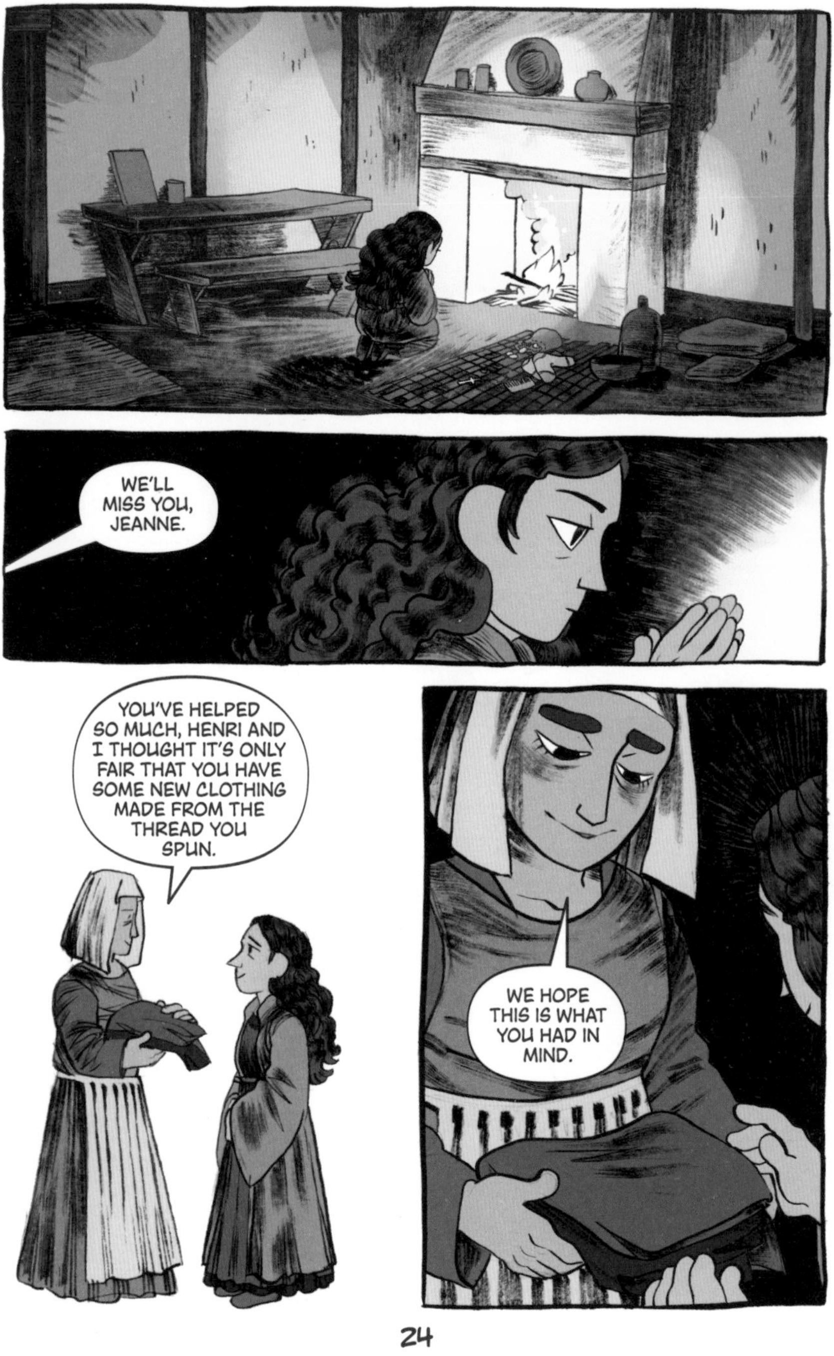

WE'LL MISS YOU, JEANNE.
YOU'VE HELPED SO MUCH, HENRI AND I THOUGHT IT'S ONLY FAIR THAT YOU HAVE SOME NEW CLOTHING MADE FROM THE THREAD YOU SPUN.
WE HOPE THIS IS WHAT YOU HAD IN MIND.

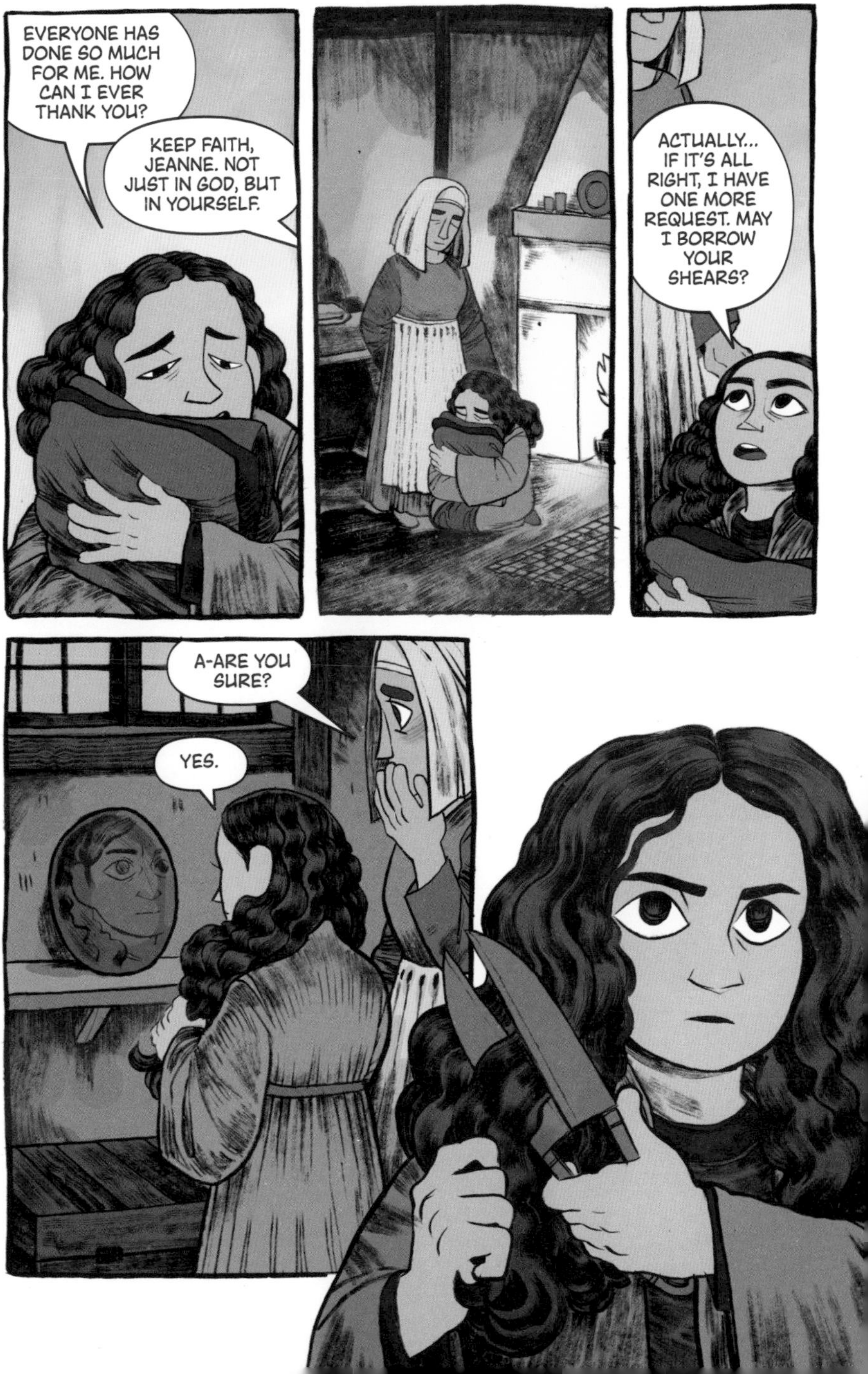
EVERYONE HAS DONE SO MUCH FOR ME. HOW CAN I EVER THANK YOU?
KEEP FAITH, JEANNE. NOT JUST IN GOD, BUT IN YOURSELF.
ACTUALLY... IF IT'S ALL RIGHT, I HAVE ONE MORE REQUEST. MAY I BORROW YOUR SHEARS?
A-ARE YOU SURE?
YES.

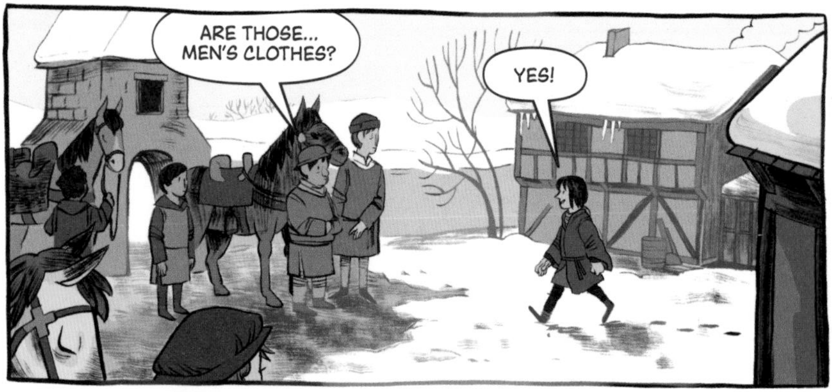
ARE THOSE... MEN'S CLOTHES?
YES!

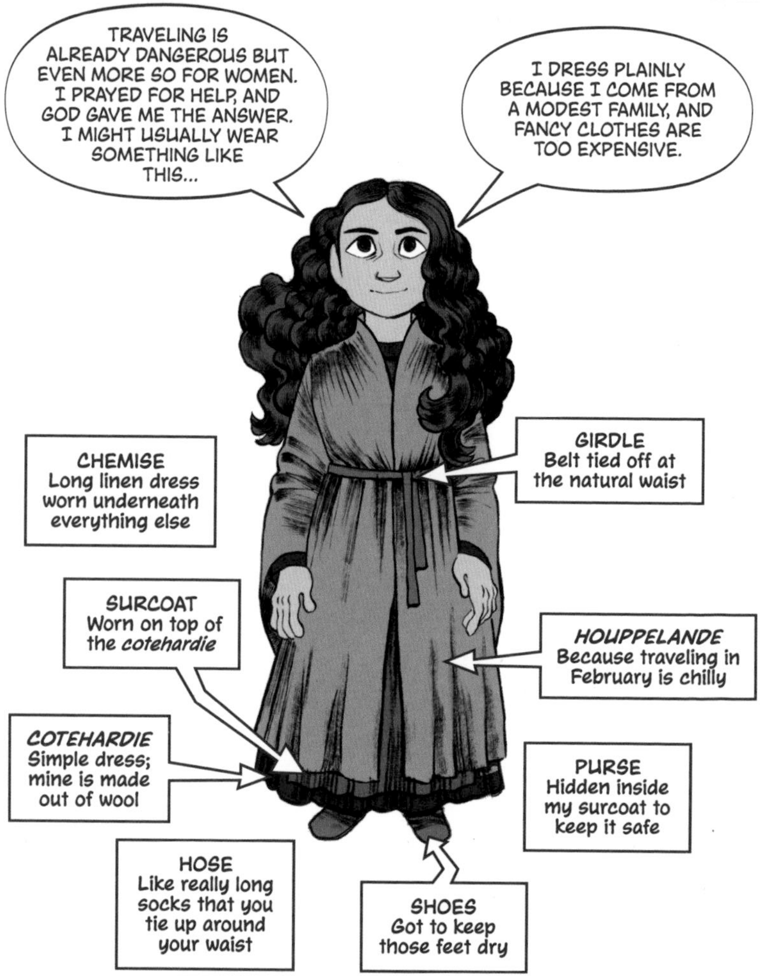
TRAVELING IS ALREADY DANGEROUS BUT EVEN MORE SO FOR WOMEN. I PRAYED FOR HELP, AND GOD GAVE ME THE ANSWER. I MIGHT USUALLY WEAR SOMETHING LIKE THIS...
I DRESS PLAINLY BECAUSE I COME FROM A MODEST FAMILY, AND FANCY CLOTHES ARE TOO EXPENSIVE.
CHEMISE Long linen dress worn underneath everything else
GIRDLE Belt tied off at the natural waist
SURCOAT Worn on top of the *cotehardie*
HOUPPELANDE Because traveling in February is chilly
COTEHARDIE Simple dress; mine is made out of wool
PURSE Hidden inside my surcoat to keep it safe
HOSE Like really long socks that you tie up around your waist
SHOES Got to keep those feet dry

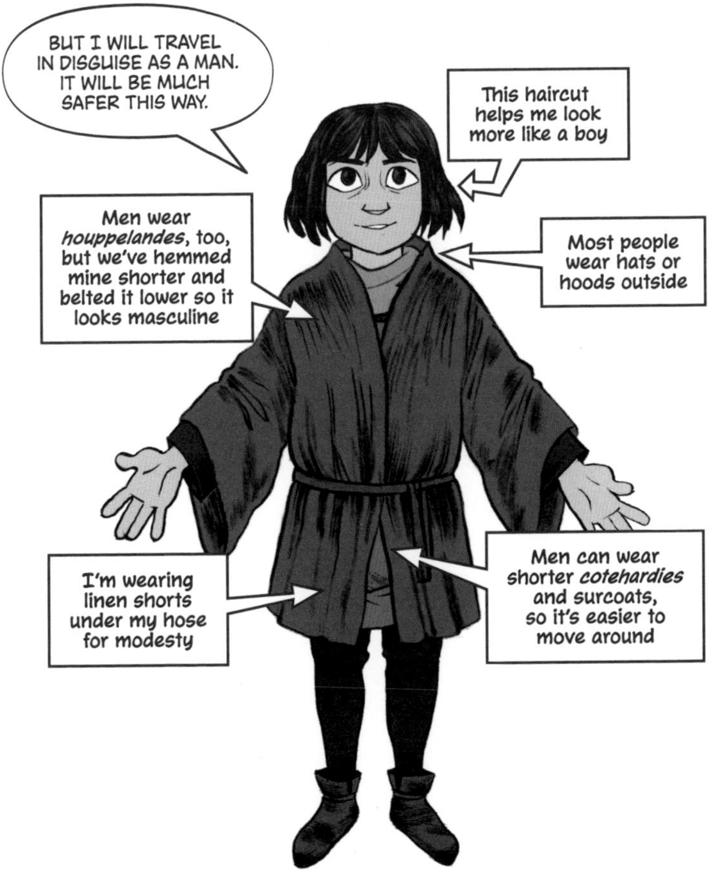
BUT I WILL TRAVEL IN DISGUISE AS A MAN. IT WILL BE MUCH SAFER THIS WAY.
This haircut helps me look more like a boy
Men wear *houppelandes*, too, but we've hemmed mine shorter and belted it lower so it looks masculine
Most people wear hats or hoods outside
I'm wearing linen shorts under my hose for modesty
Men can wear shorter *cotehardies* and surcoats, so it's easier to move around

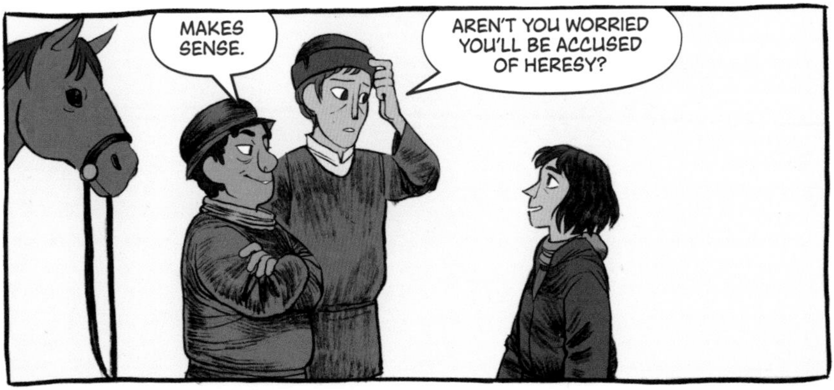
MAKES SENSE.
AREN'T YOU WORRIED YOU'LL BE ACCUSED OF HERESY?

Heresy in Catholicism

Heresy is a belief or action that goes against what is accepted in an organized religion. In the fifteenth century, the head of the Catholic Church, the pope, was the most powerful man in Europe, and Catholicism played a big part in shaping laws, governments, and people's daily lives. Anyone who didn't follow the rules of Catholicism was called a heretic, an idea that Jeanne also believed in. At the time, acts of heresy included: questioning Catholic understanding of the Bible; coming up with your own ways to observe holy days; and, sometimes, wearing clothing that didn't match your assigned gender. Heresy was punishable by prison, torture, or even death.

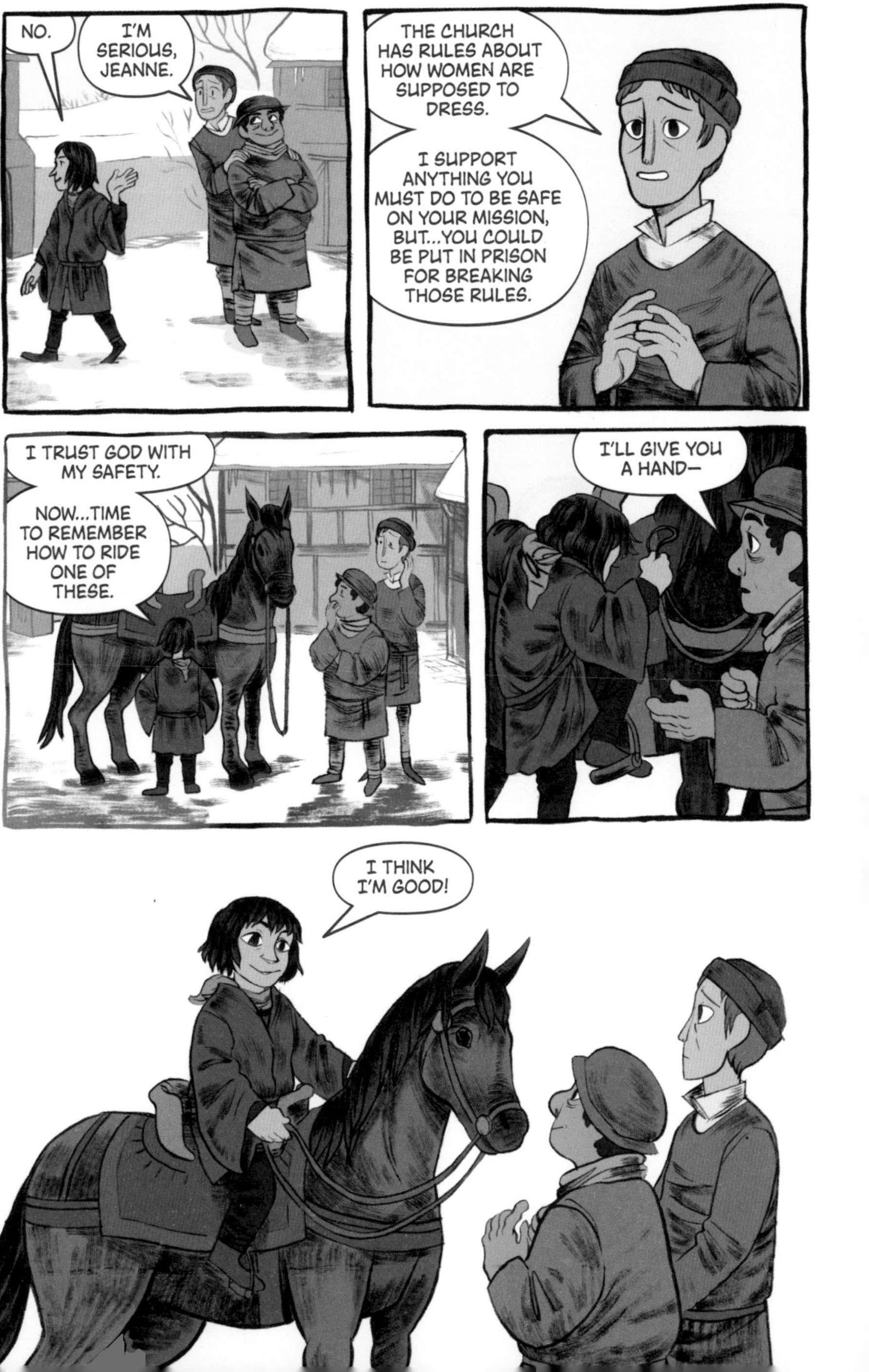
NO.
I'M SERIOUS, JEANNE.
THE CHURCH HAS RULES ABOUT HOW WOMEN ARE SUPPOSED TO DRESS.
I SUPPORT ANYTHING YOU MUST DO TO BE SAFE ON YOUR MISSION, BUT...YOU COULD BE PUT IN PRISON FOR BREAKING THOSE RULES.
I TRUST GOD WITH MY SAFETY.
NOW...TIME TO REMEMBER HOW TO RIDE ONE OF THESE.
I'LL GIVE YOU A HAND—
I THINK I'M GOOD!

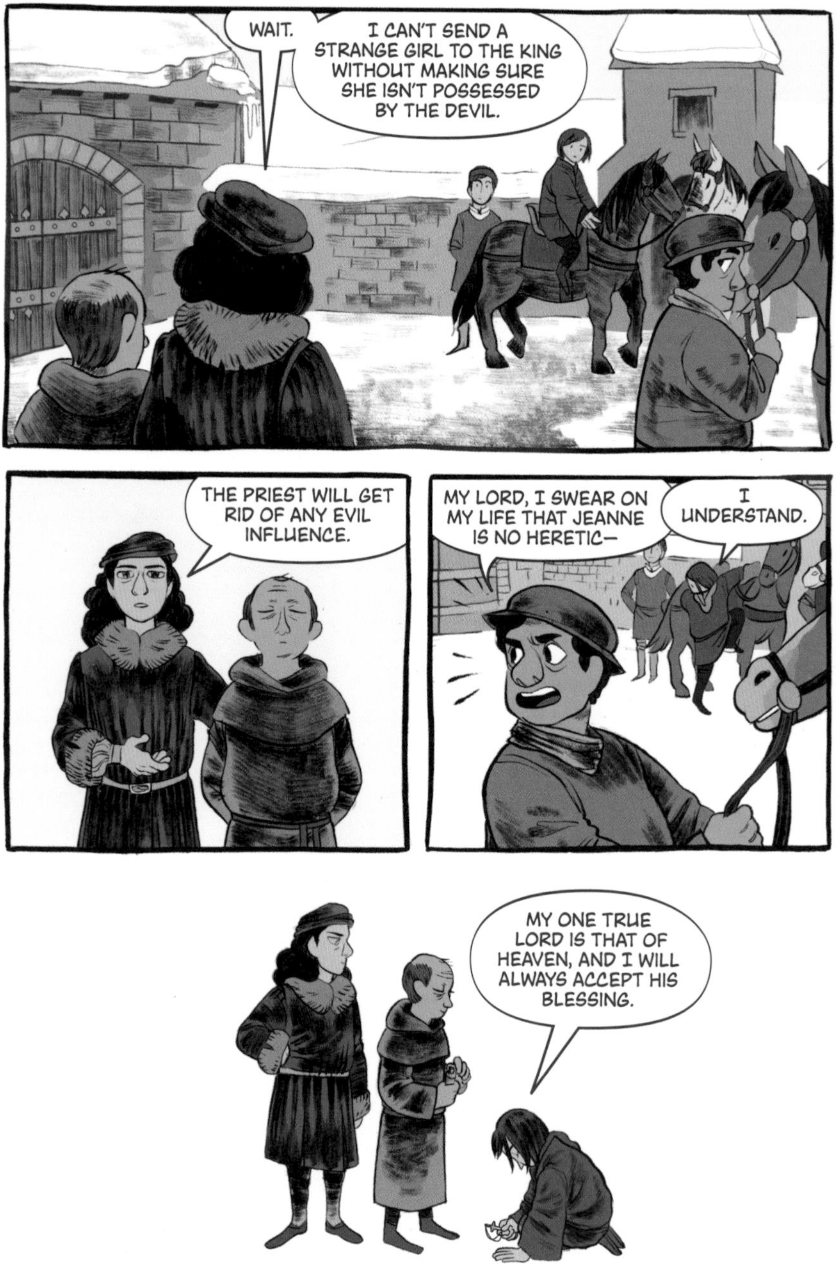
WAIT.
I CAN'T SEND A STRANGE GIRL TO THE KING WITHOUT MAKING SURE SHE ISN'T POSSESSED BY THE DEVIL.
THE PRIEST WILL GET RID OF ANY EVIL INFLUENCE.
MY LORD, I SWEAR ON MY LIFE THAT JEANNE IS NO HERETIC—
I UNDERSTAND.
MY ONE TRUE LORD IS THAT OF HEAVEN, AND I WILL ALWAYS ACCEPT HIS BLESSING.

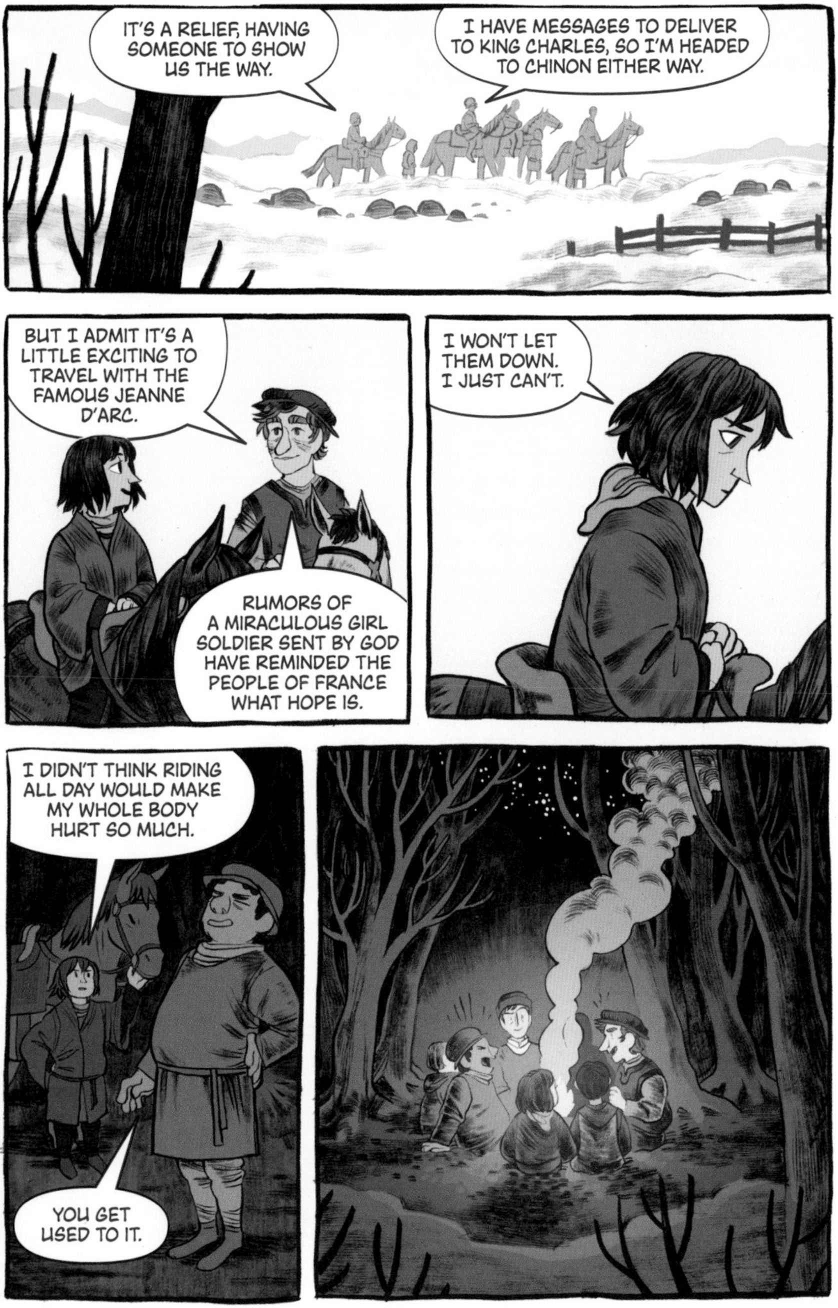
IT'S A RELIEF, HAVING SOMEONE TO SHOW US THE WAY.
I HAVE MESSAGES TO DELIVER TO KING CHARLES, SO I'M HEADED TO CHINON EITHER WAY.
BUT I ADMIT IT'S A LITTLE EXCITING TO TRAVEL WITH THE FAMOUS JEANNE D'ARC.
RUMORS OF A MIRACULOUS GIRL SOLDIER SENT BY GOD HAVE REMINDED THE PEOPLE OF FRANCE WHAT HOPE IS.
I WON'T LET THEM DOWN. I JUST CAN'T.
I DIDN'T THINK RIDING ALL DAY WOULD MAKE MY WHOLE BODY HURT SO MUCH.
YOU GET USED TO IT.

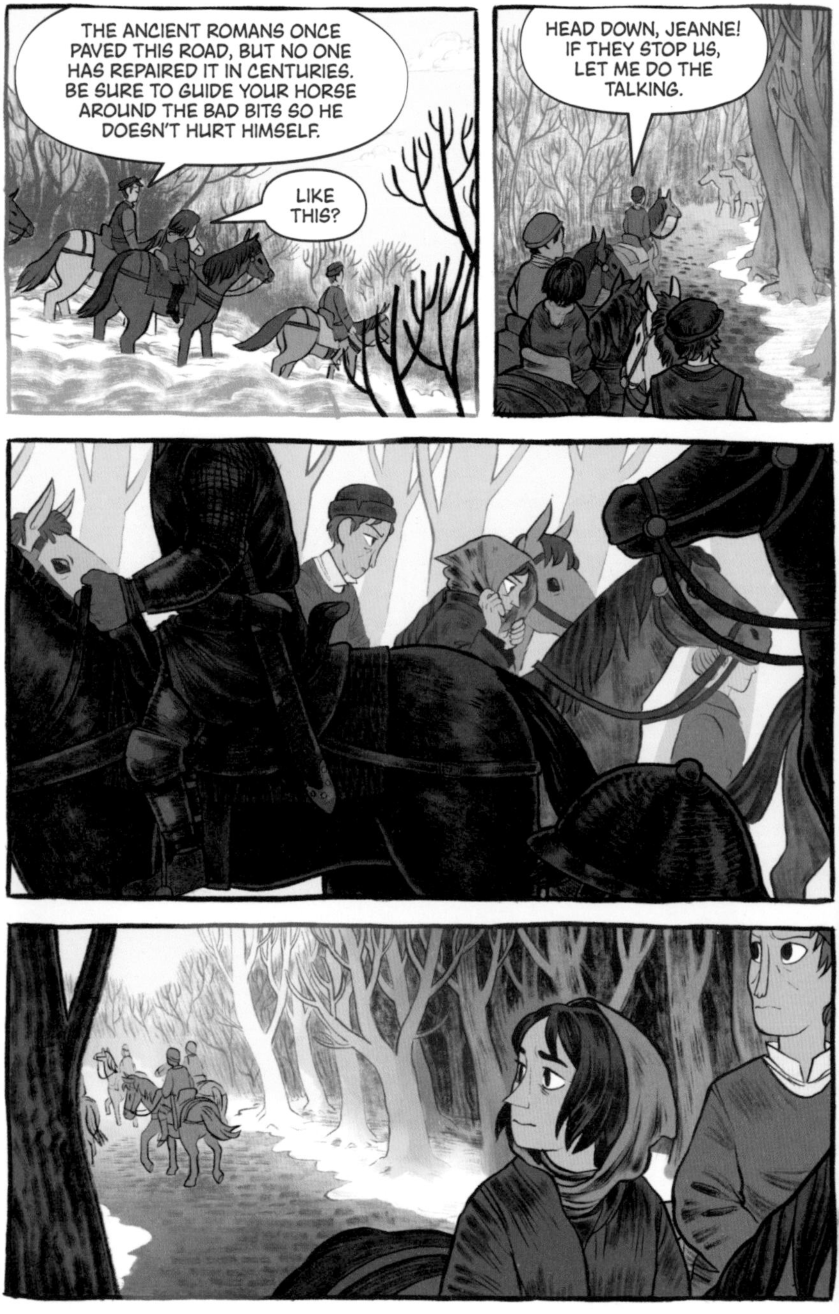

THE ANCIENT ROMANS ONCE PAVED THIS ROAD, BUT NO ONE HAS REPAIRED IT IN CENTURIES. BE SURE TO GUIDE YOUR HORSE AROUND THE BAD BITS SO HE DOESN'T HURT HIMSELF.
LIKE THIS?
HEAD DOWN, JEANNE! IF THEY STOP US, LET ME DO THE TALKING.

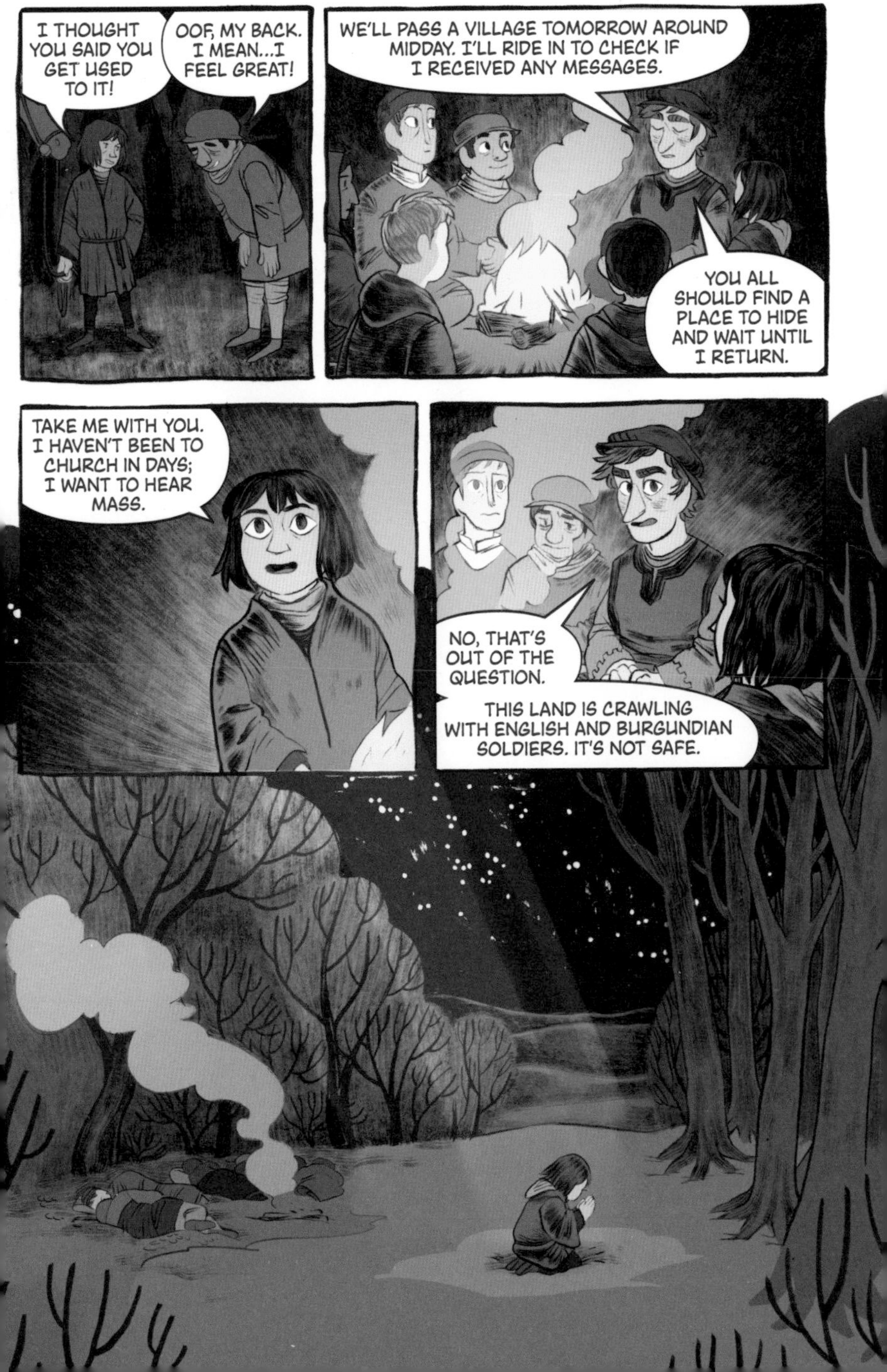
I THOUGHT YOU SAID YOU GET USED TO IT!
OOF, MY BACK. I MEAN...I FEEL GREAT!
WE'LL PASS A VILLAGE TOMORROW AROUND MIDDAY. I'LL RIDE IN TO CHECK IF I RECEIVED ANY MESSAGES.
YOU ALL SHOULD FIND A PLACE TO HIDE AND WAIT UNTIL I RETURN.
TAKE ME WITH YOU. I HAVEN'T BEEN TO CHURCH IN DAYS; I WANT TO HEAR MASS.
NO, THAT'S OUT OF THE QUESTION.
THIS LAND IS CRAWLING WITH ENGLISH AND BURGUNDIAN SOLDIERS. IT'S NOT SAFE.

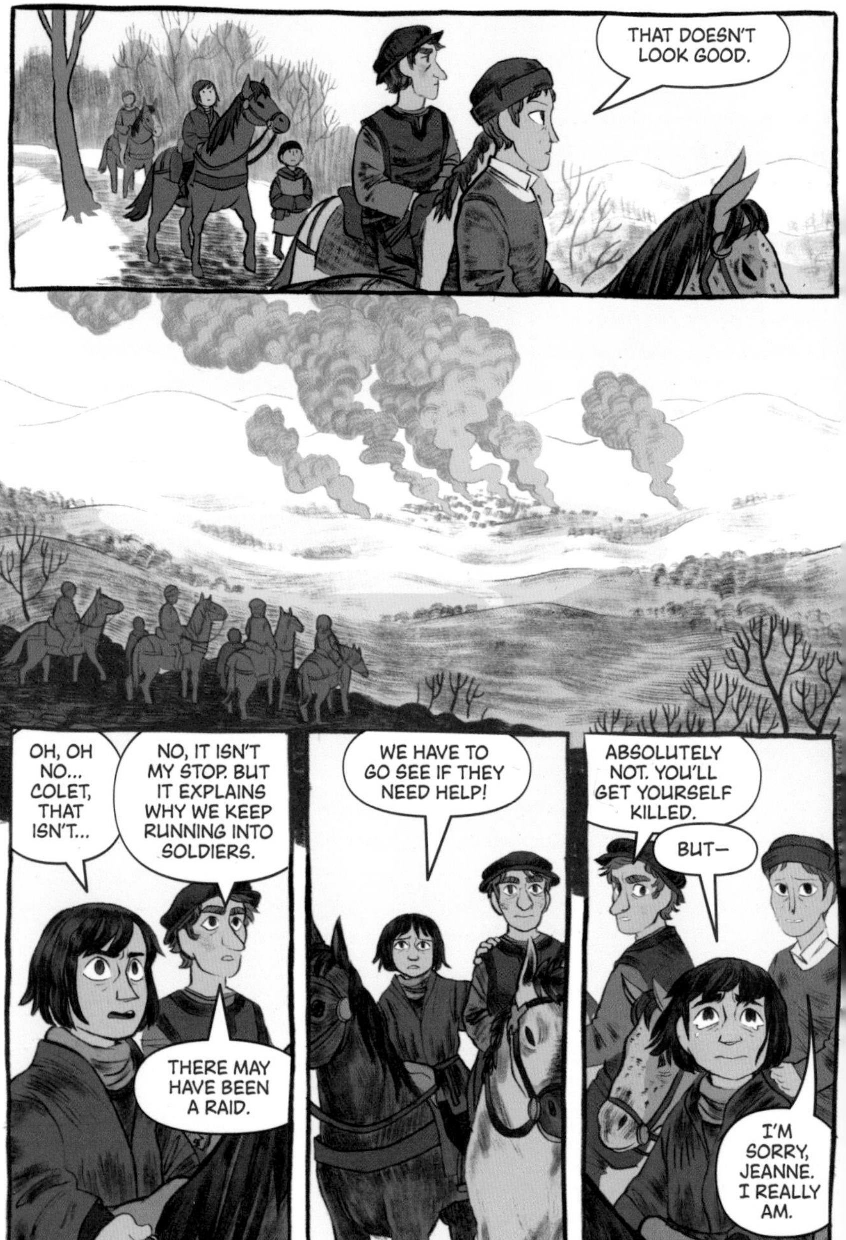
THAT DOESN'T LOOK GOOD.
OH, OH NO... COLET, THAT ISN'T...
NO, IT ISN'T MY STOP. BUT IT EXPLAINS WHY WE KEEP RUNNING INTO SOLDIERS.
THERE MAY HAVE BEEN A RAID.
WE HAVE TO GO SEE IF THEY NEED HELP!
ABSOLUTELY NOT. YOU'LL GET YOURSELF KILLED.
BUT—
I'M SORRY, JEANNE. I REALLY AM.

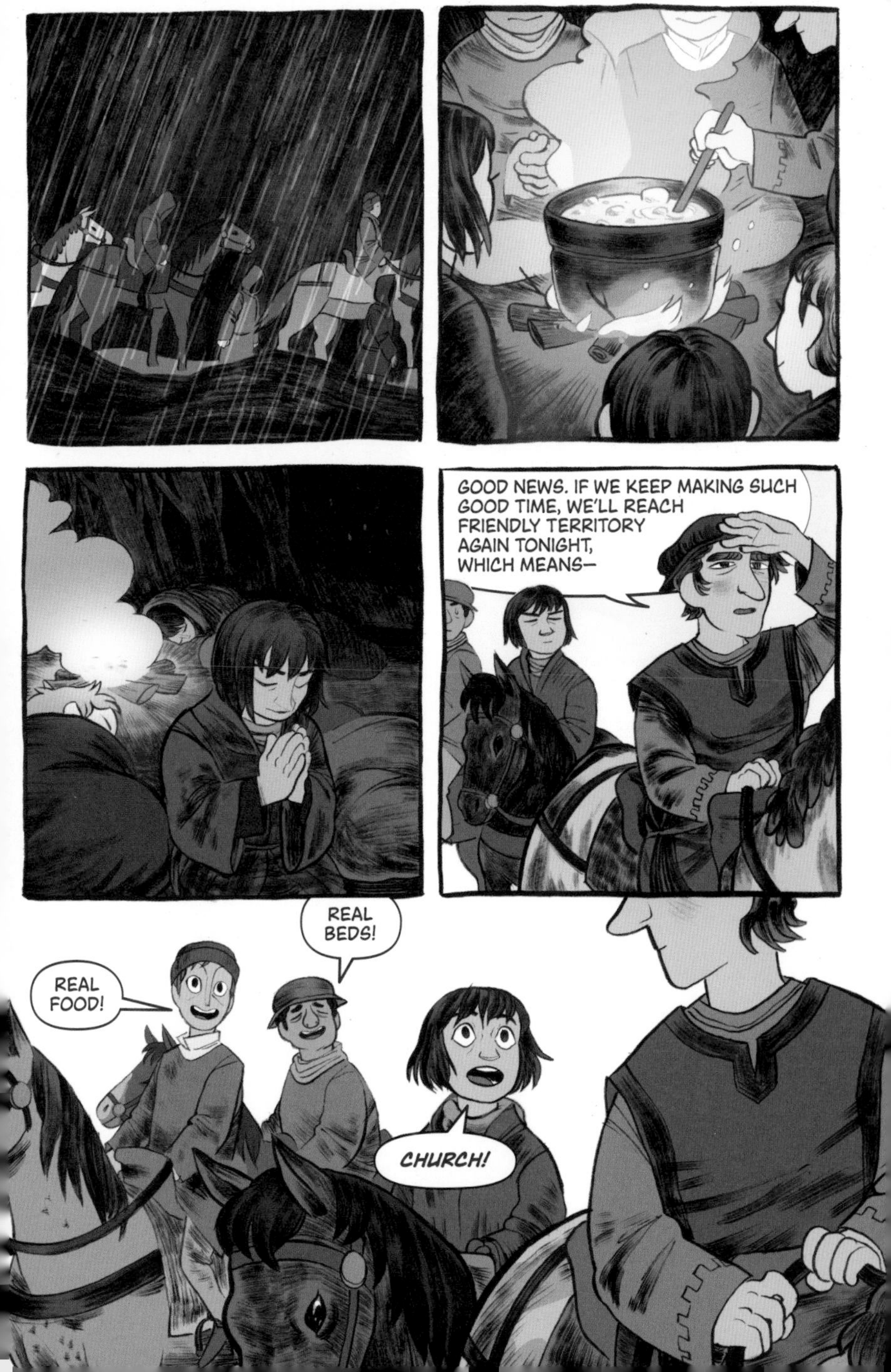
GOOD NEWS. IF WE KEEP MAKING SUCH GOOD TIME, WE'LL REACH FRIENDLY TERRITORY AGAIN TONIGHT, WHICH MEANS—
REAL FOOD!
REAL BEDS!
CHURCH!

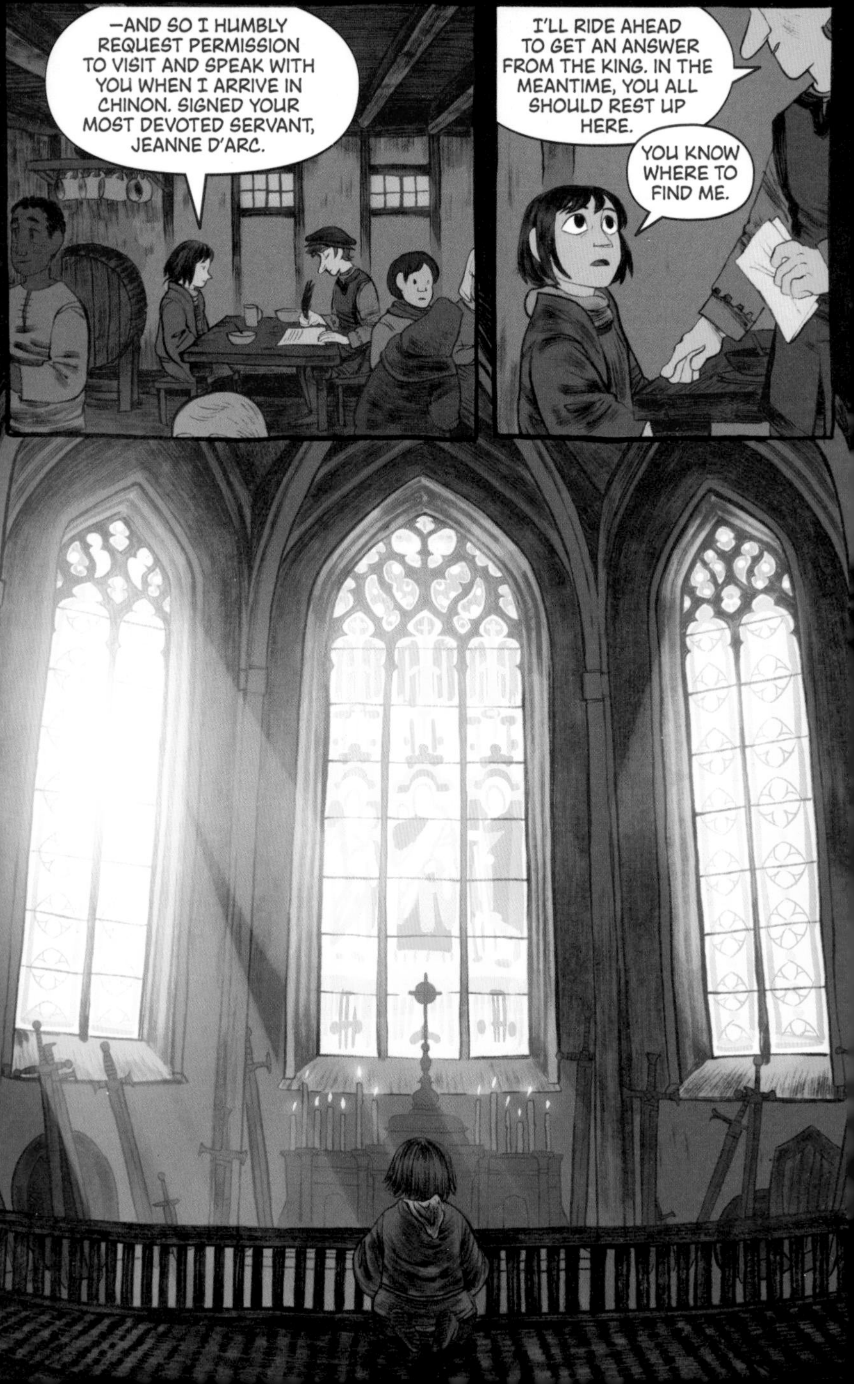
—AND SO I HUMBLY REQUEST PERMISSION TO VISIT AND SPEAK WITH YOU WHEN I ARRIVE IN CHINON. SIGNED YOUR MOST DEVOTED SERVANT, JEANNE D'ARC.
I'LL RIDE AHEAD TO GET AN ANSWER FROM THE KING. IN THE MEANTIME, YOU ALL SHOULD REST UP HERE.
YOU KNOW WHERE TO FIND ME.

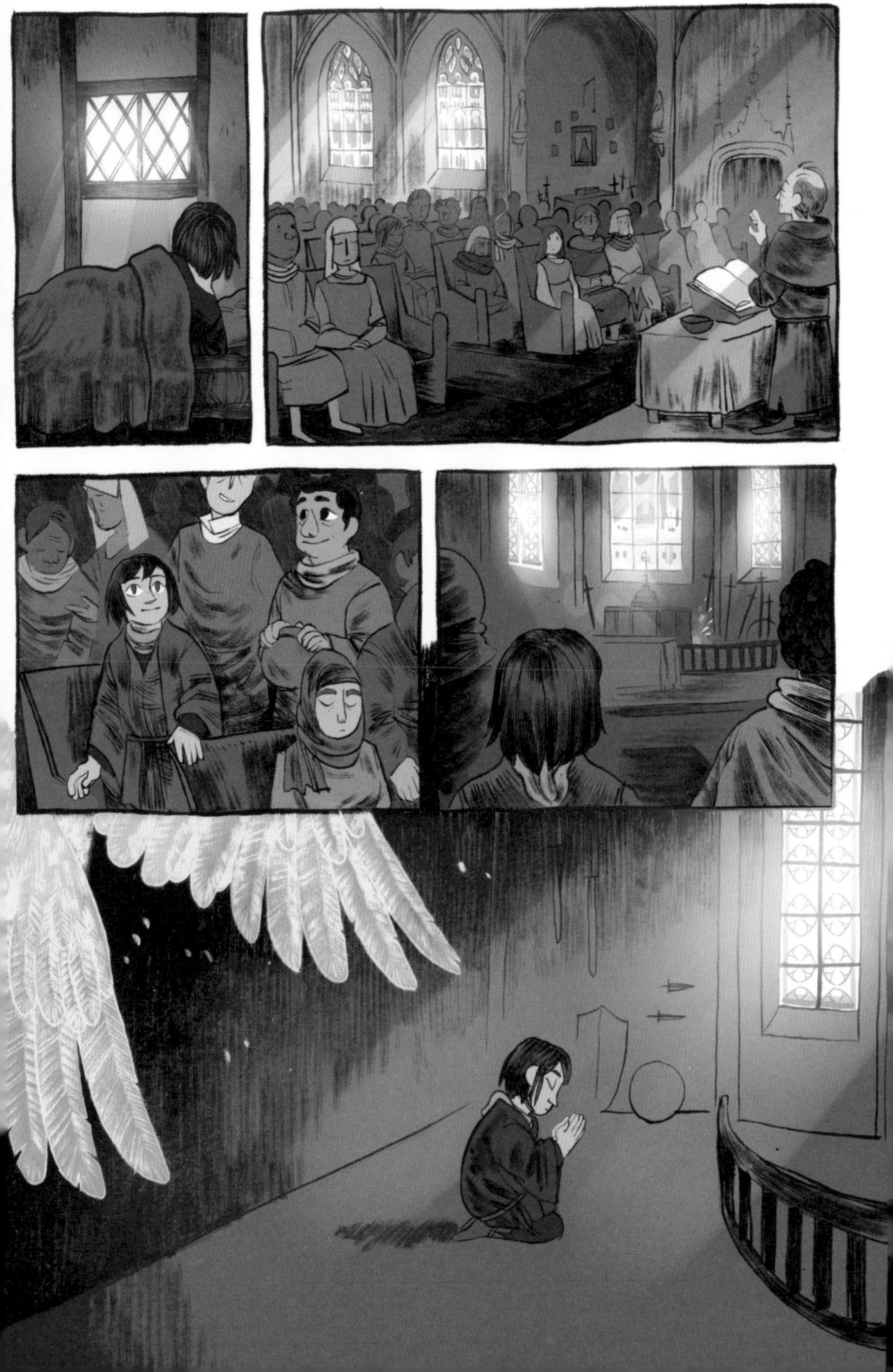

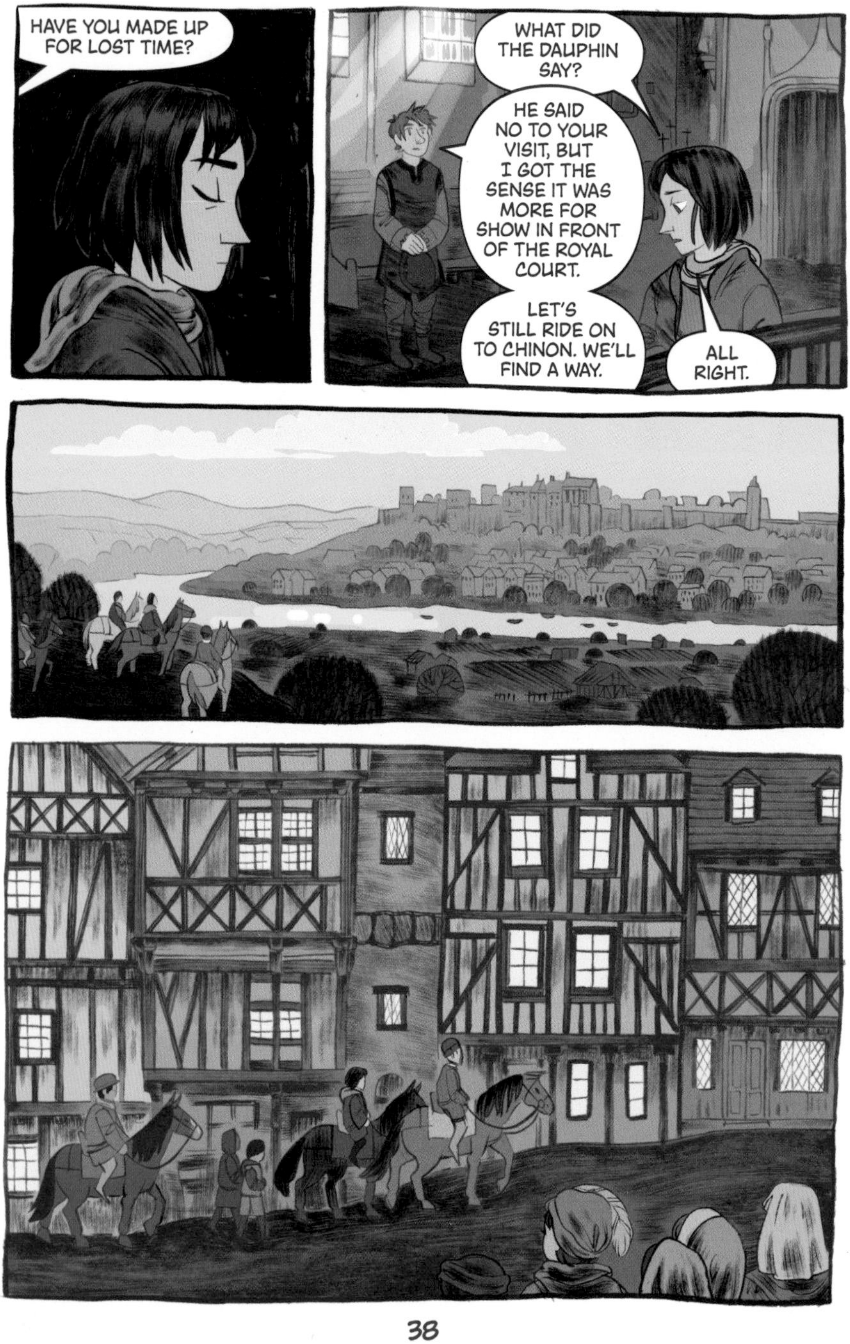
HAVE YOU MADE UP FOR LOST TIME?
WHAT DID THE DAUPHIN SAY?
HE SAID NO TO YOUR VISIT, BUT I GOT THE SENSE IT WAS MORE FOR SHOW IN FRONT OF THE ROYAL COURT.
LET'S STILL RIDE ON TO CHINON. WE'LL FIND A WAY.
ALL RIGHT.

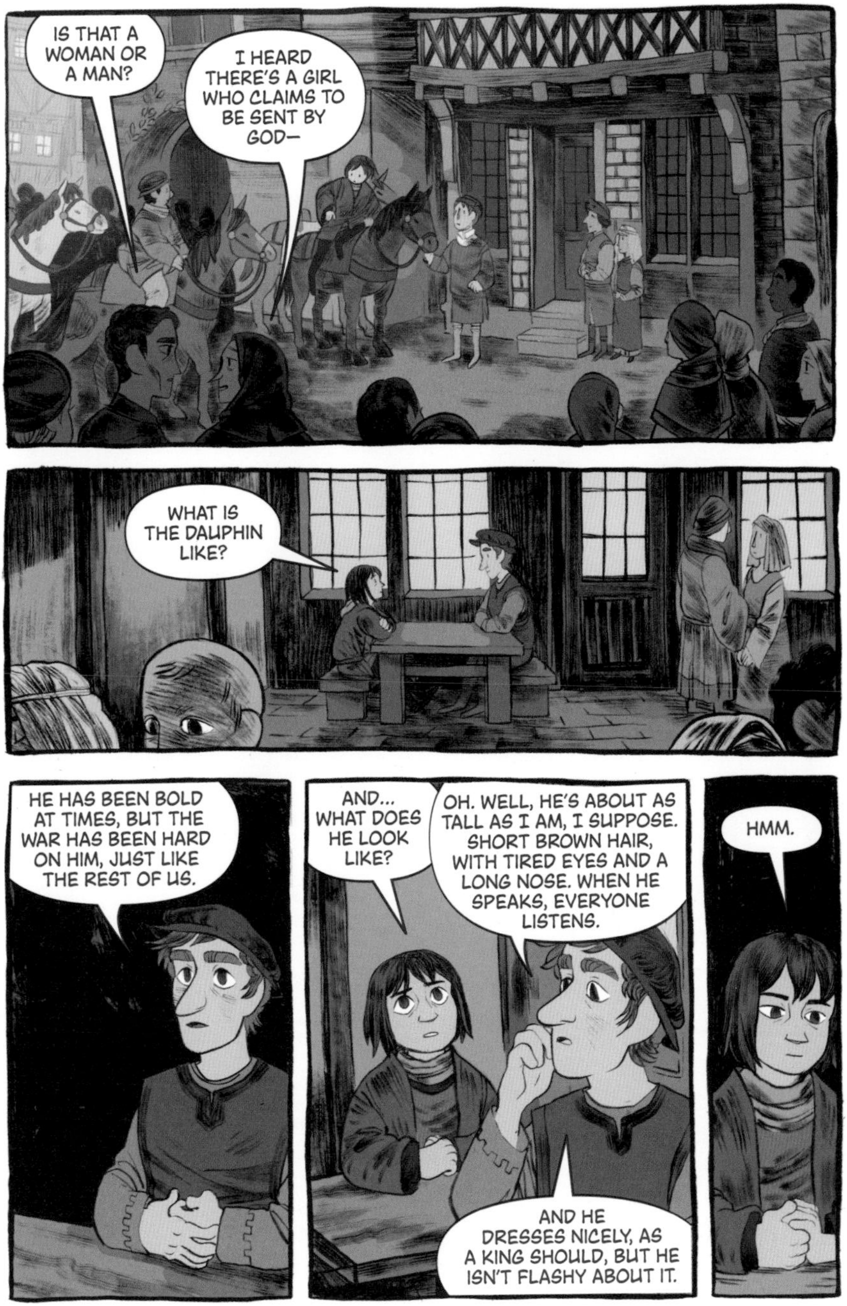
IS THAT A WOMAN OR A MAN?
I HEARD THERE'S A GIRL WHO CLAIMS TO BE SENT BY GOD—
WHAT IS THE DAUPHIN LIKE?
HE HAS BEEN BOLD AT TIMES, BUT THE WAR HAS BEEN HARD ON HIM, JUST LIKE THE REST OF US.
AND... WHAT DOES HE LOOK LIKE?
OH. WELL, HE'S ABOUT AS TALL AS I AM, I SUPPOSE. SHORT BROWN HAIR, WITH TIRED EYES AND A LONG NOSE. WHEN HE SPEAKS, EVERYONE LISTENS.
AND HE DRESSES NICELY, AS A KING SHOULD, BUT HE ISN'T FLASHY ABOUT IT.
HMM.

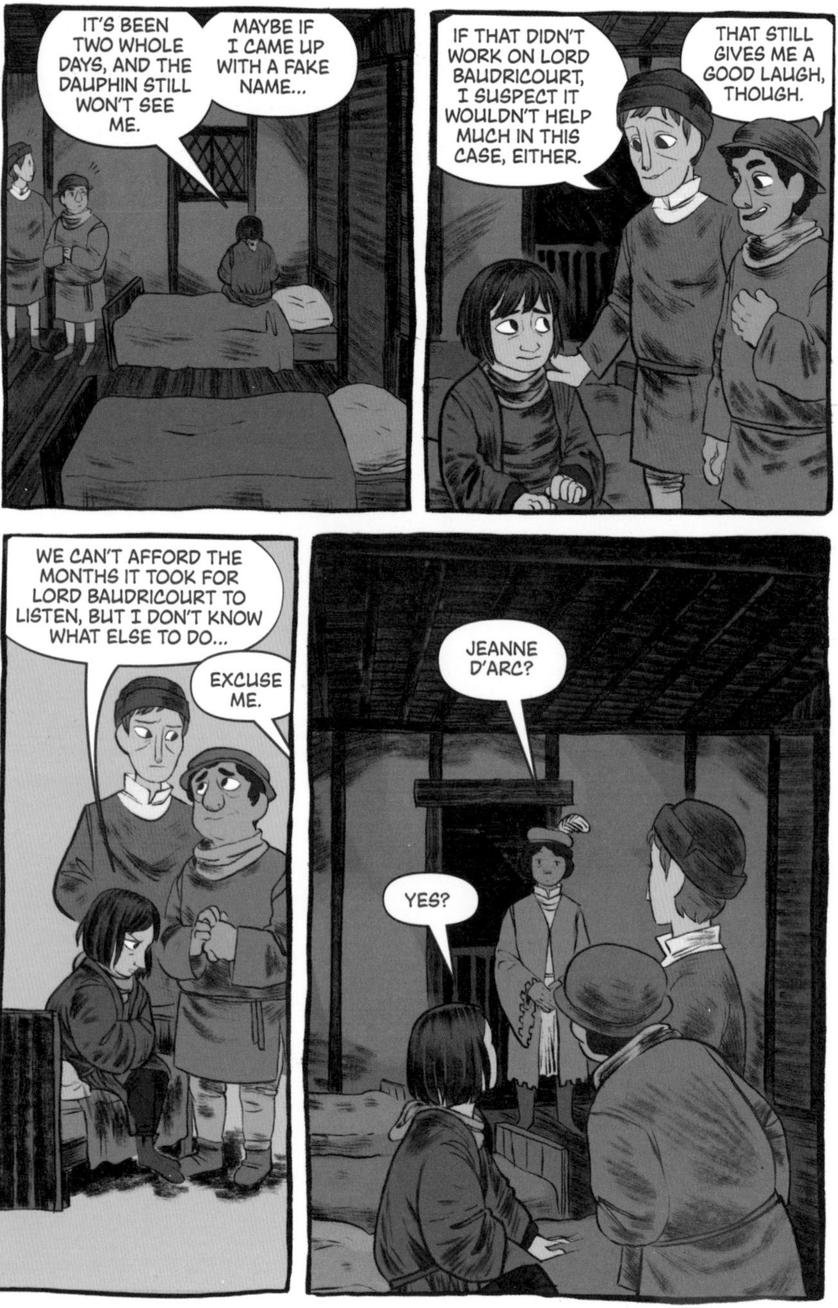
IT'S BEEN TWO WHOLE DAYS, AND THE DAUPHIN STILL WON'T SEE ME.
MAYBE IF I CAME UP WITH A FAKE NAME...
IF THAT DIDN'T WORK ON LORD BAUDRICOURT, I SUSPECT IT WOULDN'T HELP MUCH IN THIS CASE, EITHER.
THAT STILL GIVES ME A GOOD LAUGH, THOUGH.
WE CAN'T AFFORD THE MONTHS IT TOOK FOR LORD BAUDRICOURT TO LISTEN, BUT I DON'T KNOW WHAT ELSE TO DO...
EXCUSE ME.
JEANNE D'ARC?
YES?

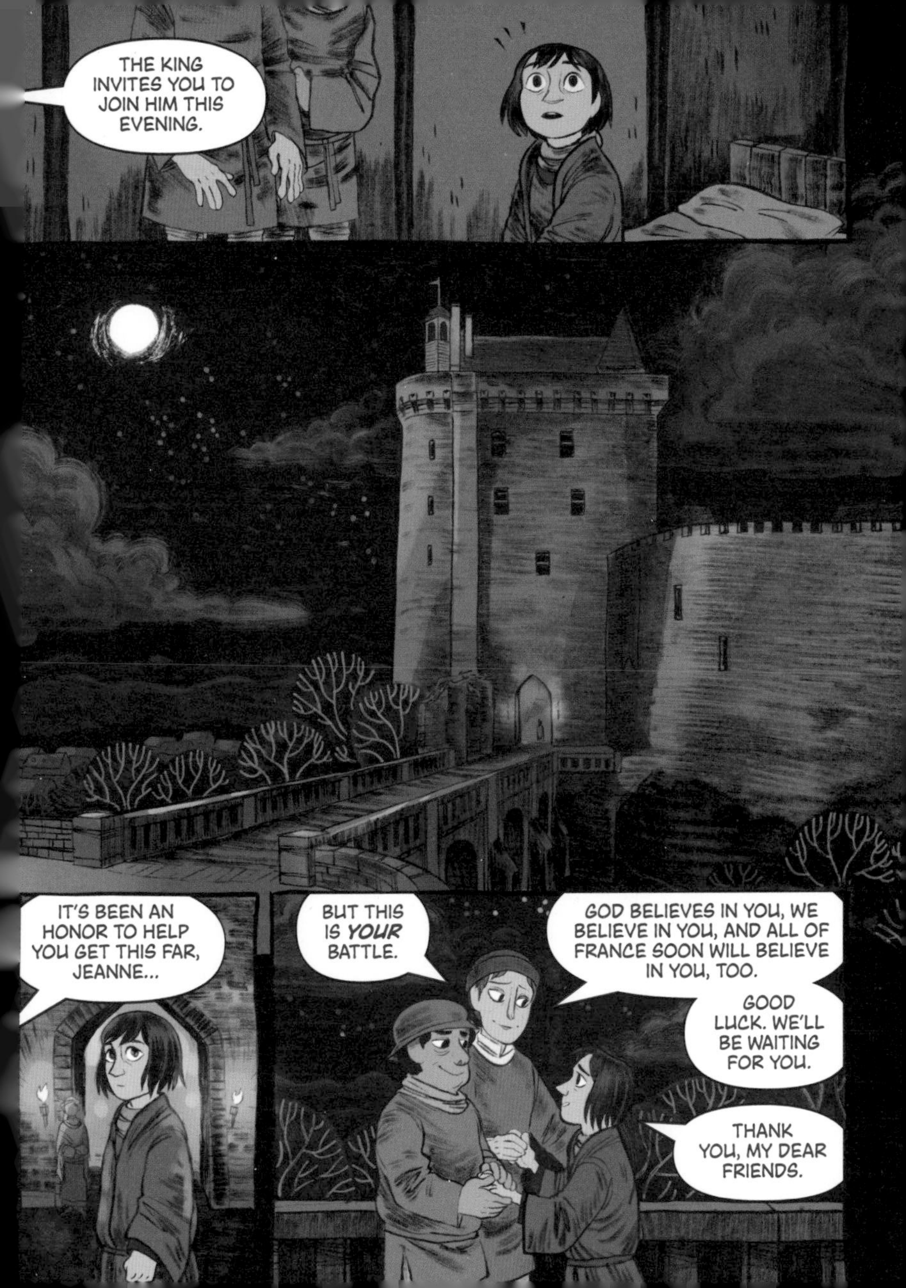
THE KING INVITES YOU TO JOIN HIM THIS EVENING.
IT'S BEEN AN HONOR TO HELP YOU GET THIS FAR, JEANNE...
BUT THIS IS *YOUR* BATTLE.
GOD BELIEVES IN YOU, WE BELIEVE IN YOU, AND ALL OF FRANCE SOON WILL BELIEVE IN YOU, TOO.
GOOD LUCK. WE'LL BE WAITING FOR YOU.
THANK YOU, MY DEAR FRIENDS.

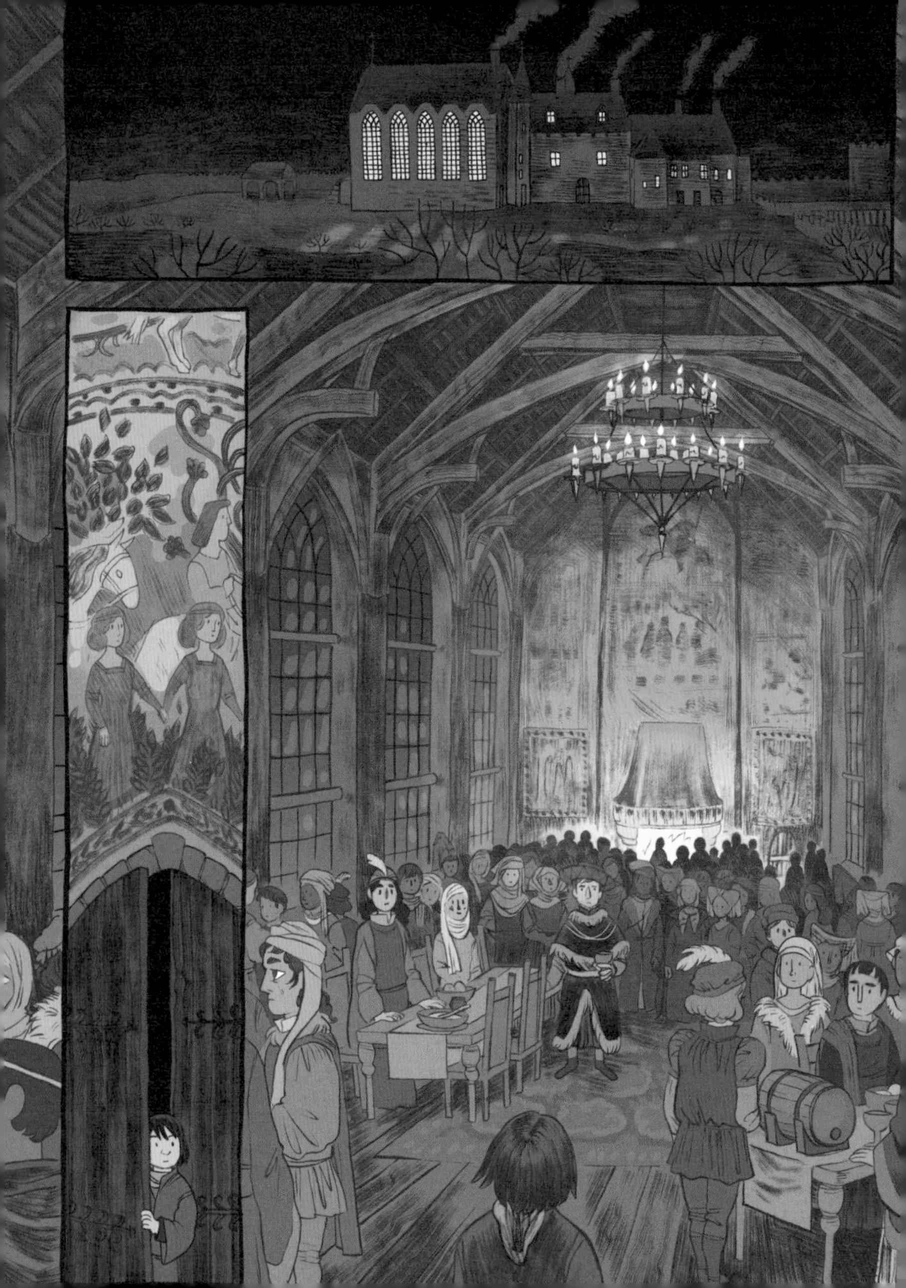

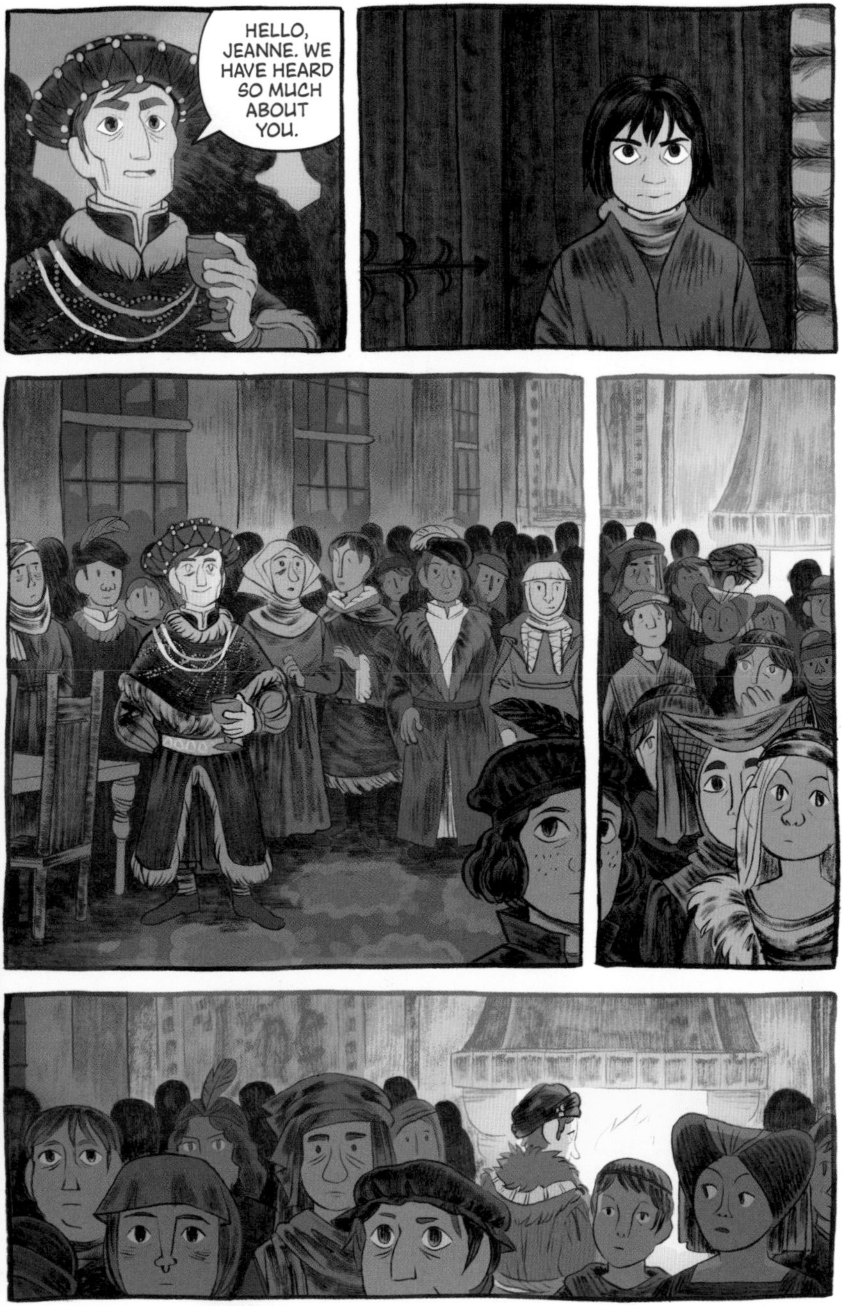
HELLO, JEANNE. WE HAVE HEARD SO MUCH ABOUT YOU.

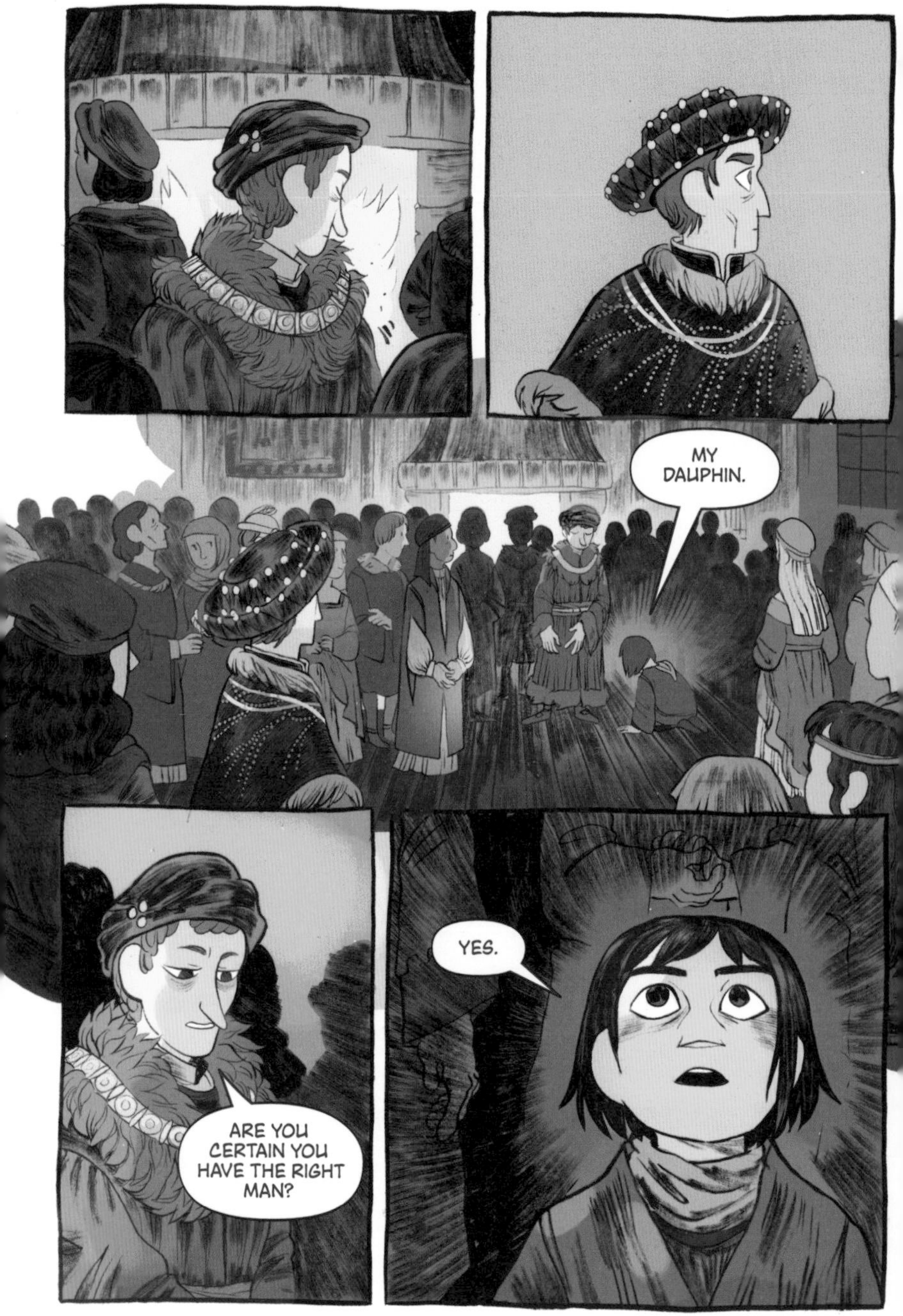
MY DAUPHIN.
ARE YOU CERTAIN YOU HAVE THE RIGHT MAN?
YES.

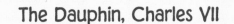

The Dauphin, Charles VII

Born in 1403, Charles VII was the son of Charles VI, who was also known as the mad king of France. Charles VII succeeded in eventually freeing France from English rule in the Hundred Years' War and reestablishing the French monarchy. Before he was crowned king, Charles VII was known as the dauphin, which is a fancy title France gave its first heir to the throne. It means *dolphin* in French, an animal that the first dauphin, Guigues IV, wore on his coat of arms.

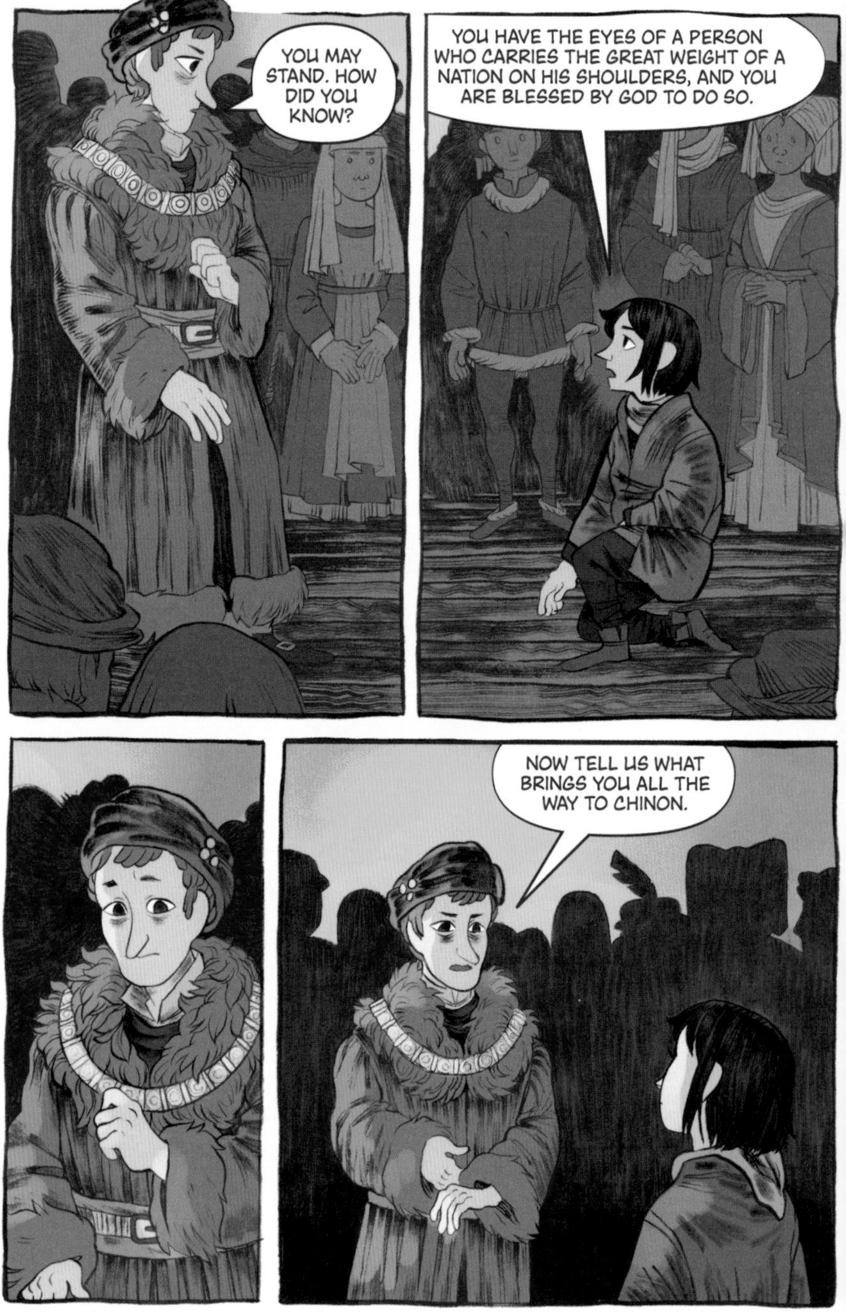
YOU MAY STAND. HOW DID YOU KNOW?
YOU HAVE THE EYES OF A PERSON WHO CARRIES THE GREAT WEIGHT OF A NATION ON HIS SHOULDERS, AND YOU ARE BLESSED BY GOD TO DO SO.
NOW TELL US WHAT BRINGS YOU ALL THE WAY TO CHINON.

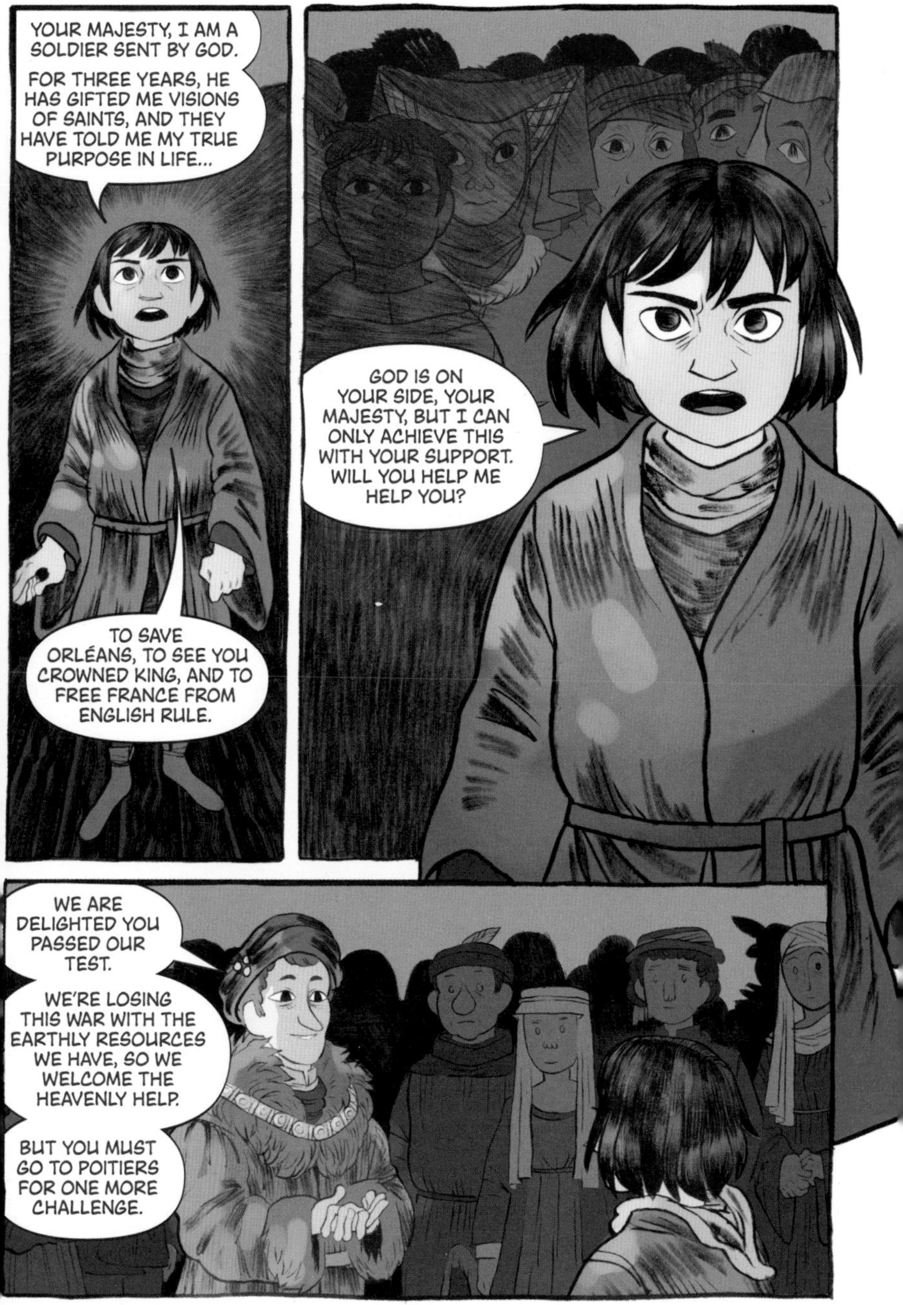
YOUR MAJESTY, I AM A SOLDIER SENT BY GOD.
FOR THREE YEARS, HE HAS GIFTED ME VISIONS OF SAINTS, AND THEY HAVE TOLD ME MY TRUE PURPOSE IN LIFE...
TO SAVE ORLÉANS, TO SEE YOU CROWNED KING, AND TO FREE FRANCE FROM ENGLISH RULE.
GOD IS ON YOUR SIDE, YOUR MAJESTY, BUT I CAN ONLY ACHIEVE THIS WITH YOUR SUPPORT. WILL YOU HELP ME HELP YOU?
WE ARE DELIGHTED YOU PASSED OUR TEST.
WE'RE LOSING THIS WAR WITH THE EARTHLY RESOURCES WE HAVE, SO WE WELCOME THE HEAVENLY HELP.
BUT YOU MUST GO TO POITIERS FOR ONE MORE CHALLENGE.

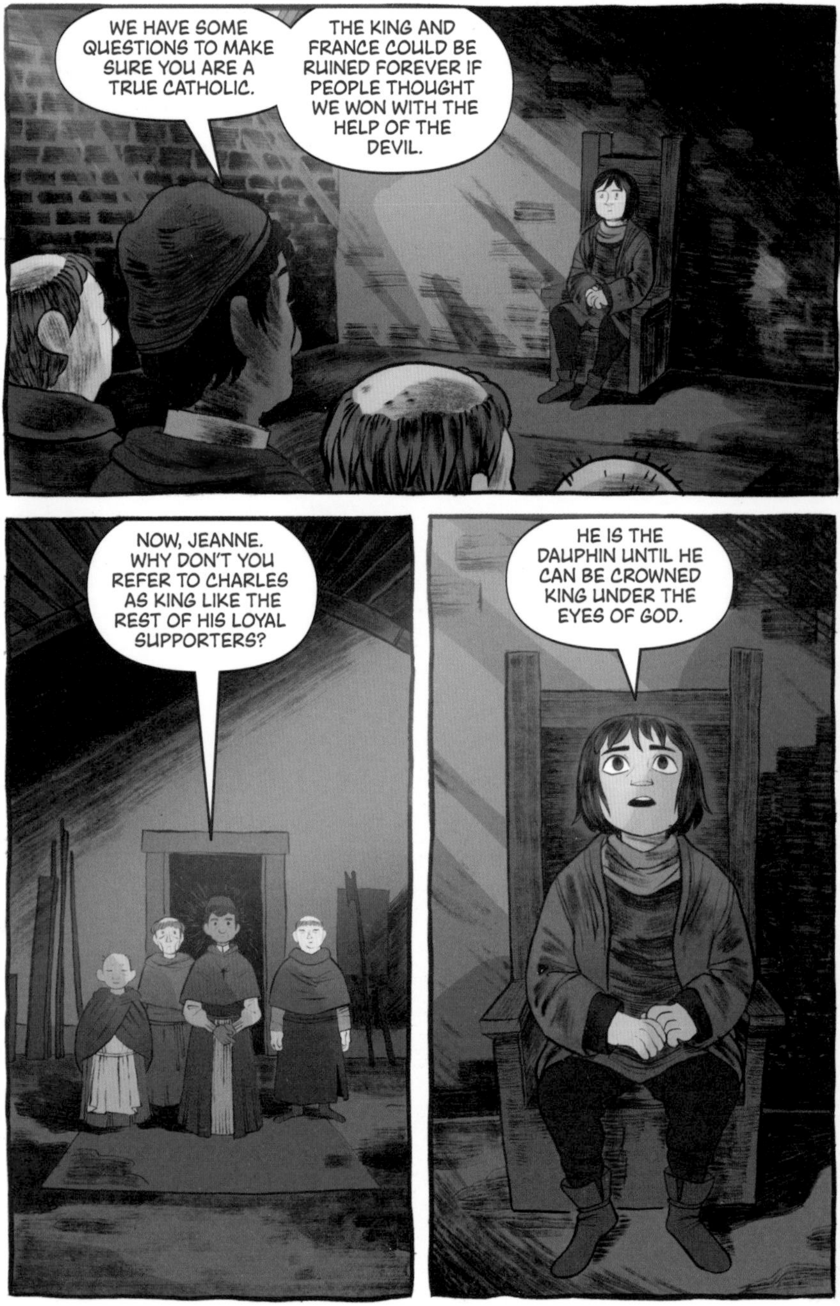
WE HAVE SOME QUESTIONS TO MAKE SURE YOU ARE A TRUE CATHOLIC.
THE KING AND FRANCE COULD BE RUINED FOREVER IF PEOPLE THOUGHT WE WON WITH THE HELP OF THE DEVIL.
NOW, JEANNE. WHY DON'T YOU REFER TO CHARLES AS KING LIKE THE REST OF HIS LOYAL SUPPORTERS?
HE IS THE DAUPHIN UNTIL HE CAN BE CROWNED KING UNDER THE EYES OF GOD.

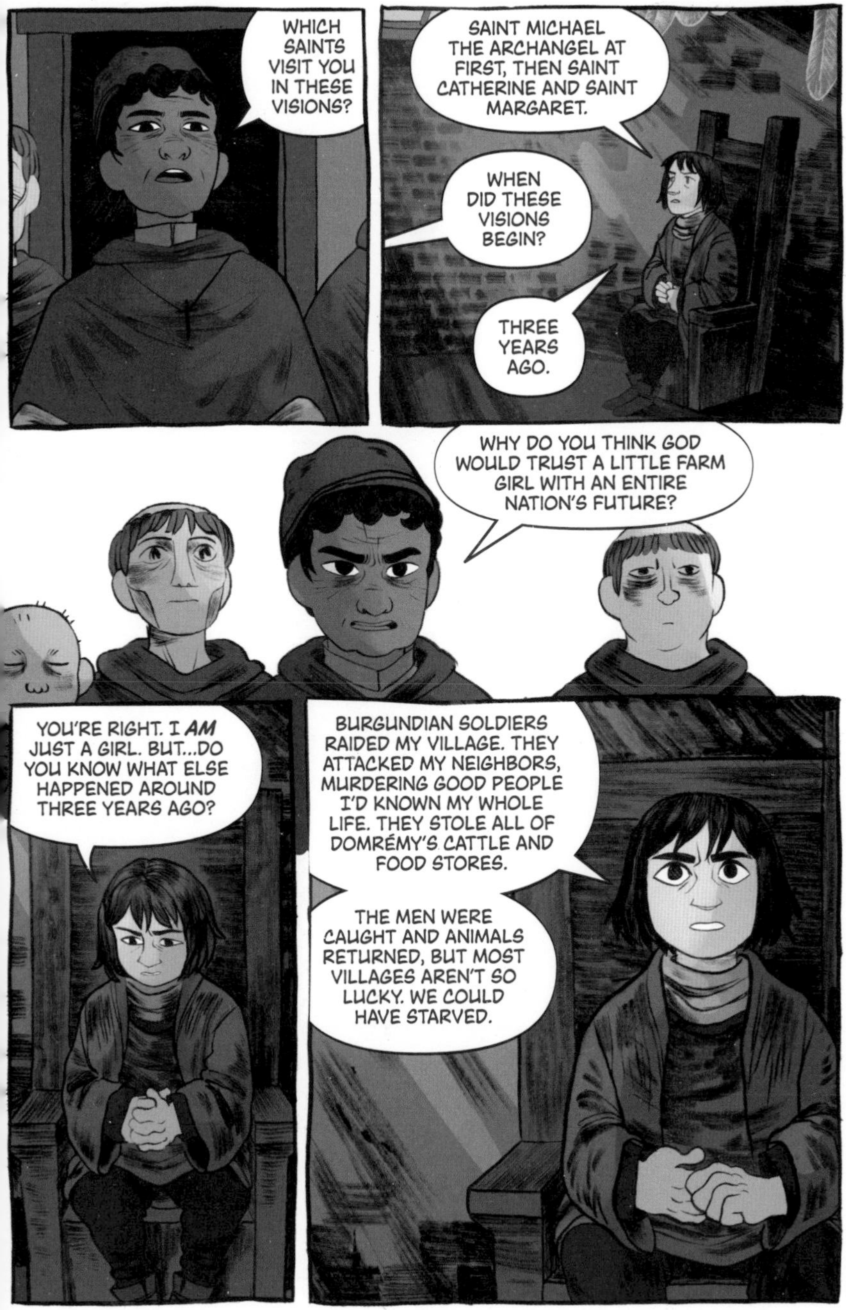
WHICH SAINTS VISIT YOU IN THESE VISIONS?
SAINT MICHAEL THE ARCHANGEL AT FIRST, THEN SAINT CATHERINE AND SAINT MARGARET.
WHEN DID THESE VISIONS BEGIN?
THREE YEARS AGO.
WHY DO YOU THINK GOD WOULD TRUST A LITTLE FARM GIRL WITH AN ENTIRE NATION'S FUTURE?
YOU'RE RIGHT. I *AM* JUST A GIRL. BUT...DO YOU KNOW WHAT ELSE HAPPENED AROUND THREE YEARS AGO?
BURGUNDIAN SOLDIERS RAIDED MY VILLAGE. THEY ATTACKED MY NEIGHBORS, MURDERING GOOD PEOPLE I'D KNOWN MY WHOLE LIFE. THEY STOLE ALL OF DOMRÉMY'S CATTLE AND FOOD STORES.
THE MEN WERE CAUGHT AND ANIMALS RETURNED, BUT MOST VILLAGES AREN'T SO LUCKY. WE COULD HAVE STARVED.

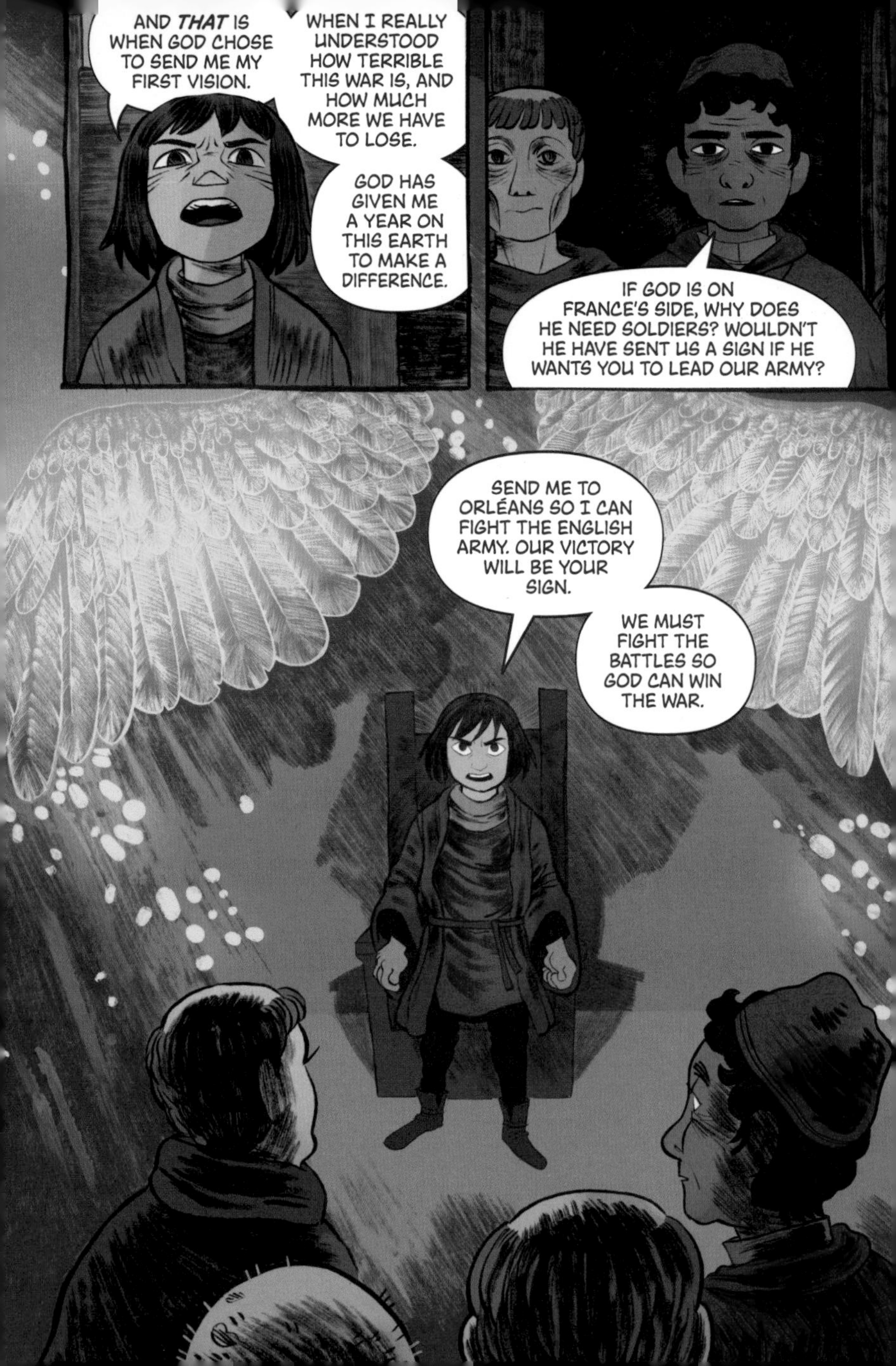
AND THAT IS WHEN GOD CHOSE TO SEND ME MY FIRST VISION.
WHEN I REALLY UNDERSTOOD HOW TERRIBLE THIS WAR IS, AND HOW MUCH MORE WE HAVE TO LOSE.
GOD HAS GIVEN ME A YEAR ON THIS EARTH TO MAKE A DIFFERENCE.
IF GOD IS ON FRANCE'S SIDE, WHY DOES HE NEED SOLDIERS? WOULDN'T HE HAVE SENT US A SIGN IF HE WANTS YOU TO LEAD OUR ARMY?
SEND ME TO ORLÉANS SO I CAN FIGHT THE ENGLISH ARMY. OUR VICTORY WILL BE YOUR SIGN.
WE MUST FIGHT THE BATTLES SO GOD CAN WIN THE WAR.

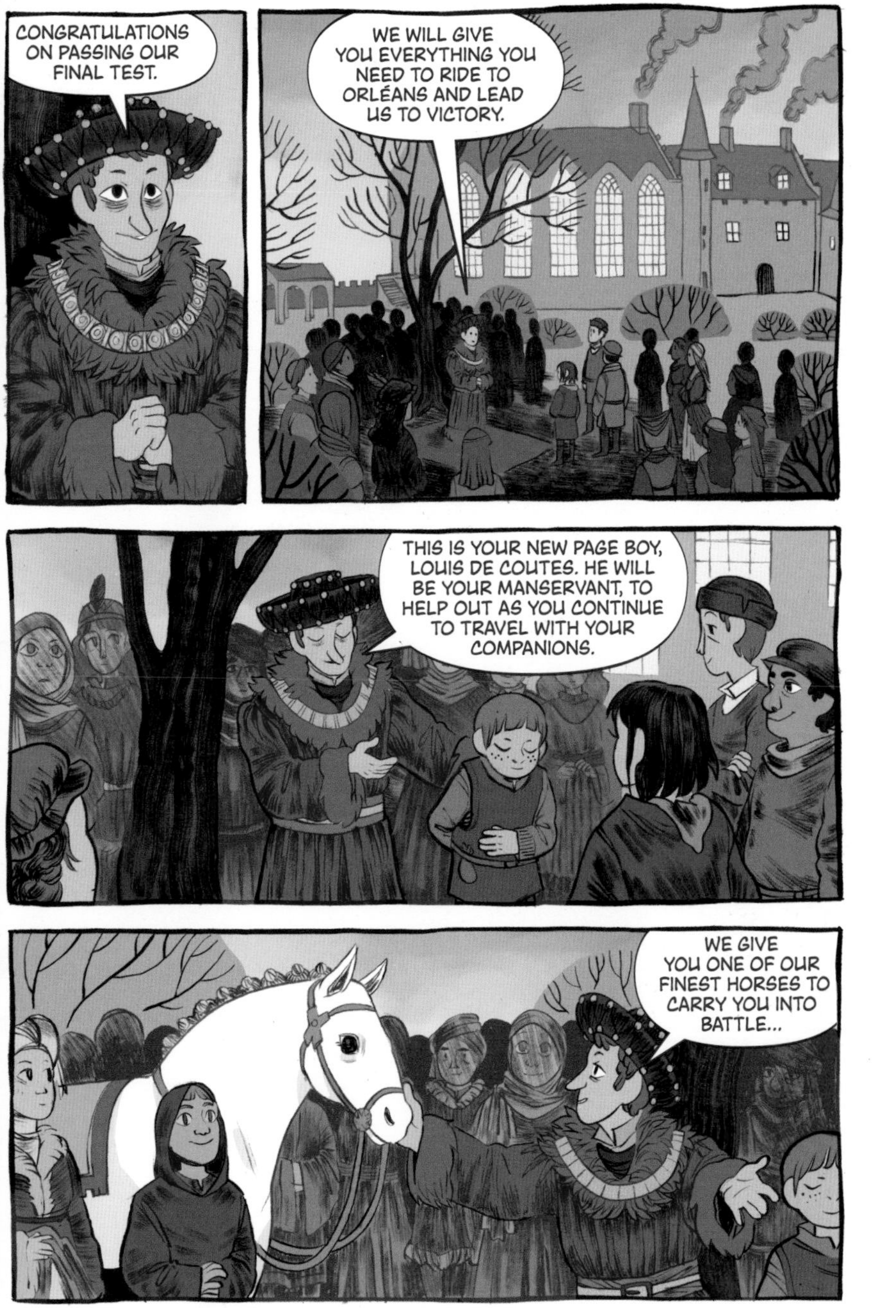
CONGRATULATIONS ON PASSING OUR FINAL TEST.
WE WILL GIVE YOU EVERYTHING YOU NEED TO RIDE TO ORLÉANS AND LEAD US TO VICTORY.
THIS IS YOUR NEW PAGE BOY, LOUIS DE COUTES. HE WILL BE YOUR MANSERVANT, TO HELP OUT AS YOU CONTINUE TO TRAVEL WITH YOUR COMPANIONS.
WE GIVE YOU ONE OF OUR FINEST HORSES TO CARRY YOU INTO BATTLE...

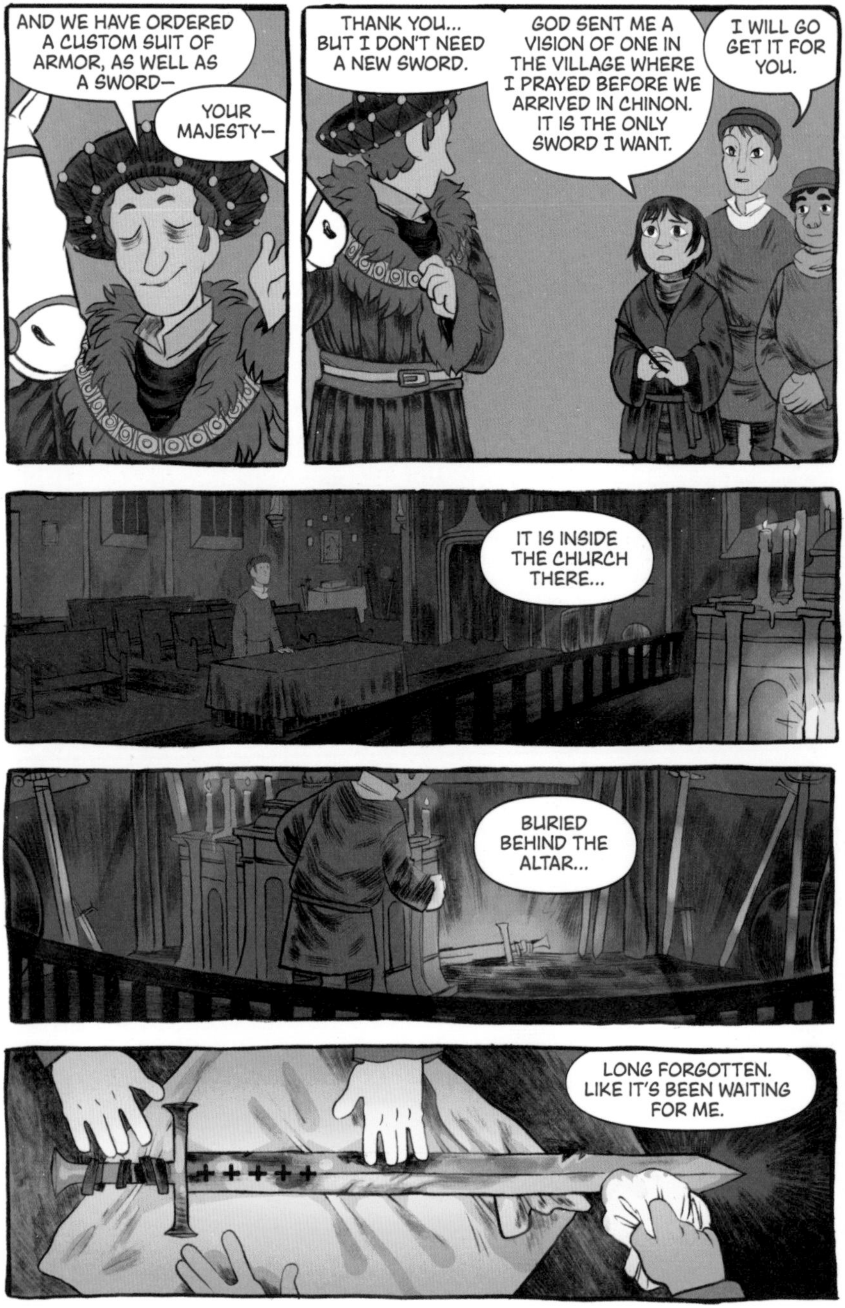
AND WE HAVE ORDERED A CUSTOM SUIT OF ARMOR, AS WELL AS A SWORD—
YOUR MAJESTY—
THANK YOU... BUT I DON'T NEED A NEW SWORD.
GOD SENT ME A VISION OF ONE IN THE VILLAGE WHERE I PRAYED BEFORE WE ARRIVED IN CHINON. IT IS THE ONLY SWORD I WANT.
I WILL GO GET IT FOR YOU.
IT IS INSIDE THE CHURCH THERE...
BURIED BEHIND THE ALTAR...
LONG FORGOTTEN. LIKE IT'S BEEN WAITING FOR ME.

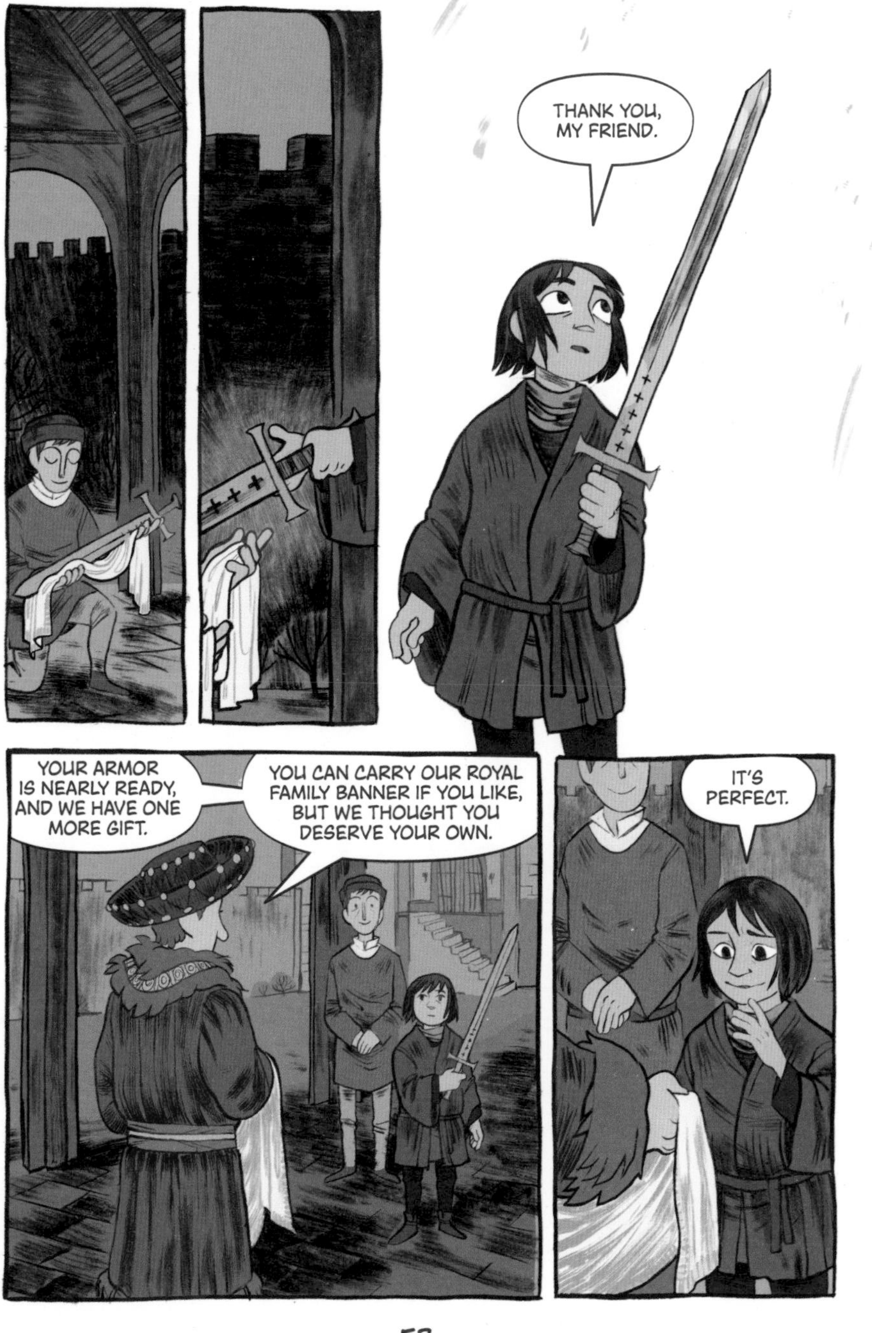
THANK YOU, MY FRIEND.
YOUR ARMOR IS NEARLY READY, AND WE HAVE ONE MORE GIFT.
YOU CAN CARRY OUR ROYAL FAMILY BANNER IF YOU LIKE, BUT WE THOUGHT YOU DESERVE YOUR OWN.
IT'S PERFECT.

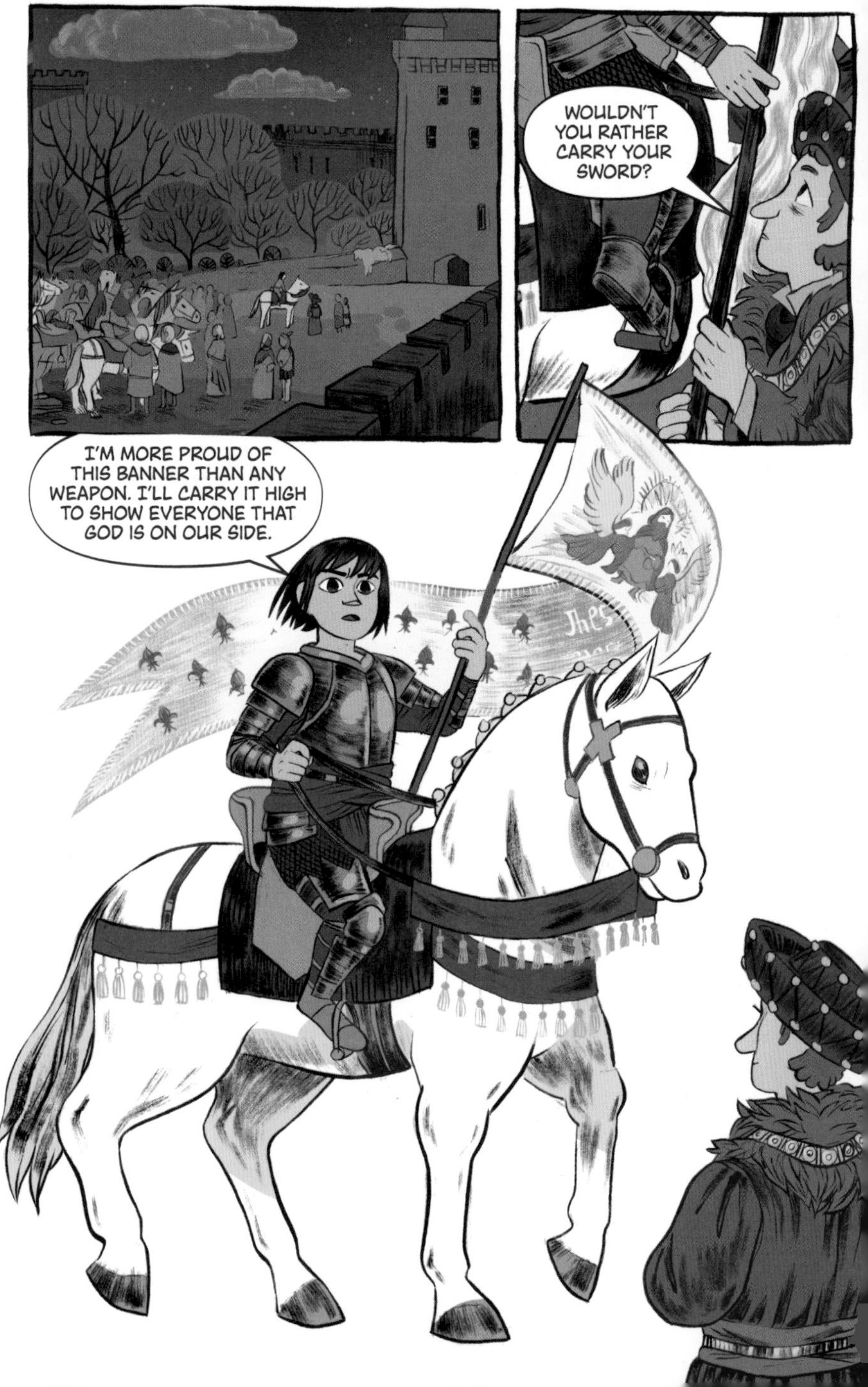
WOULDN'T YOU RATHER CARRY YOUR SWORD?
I'M MORE PROUD OF THIS BANNER THAN ANY WEAPON. I'LL CARRY IT HIGH TO SHOW EVERYONE THAT GOD IS ON OUR SIDE.

Sainthood

In the Catholic religion, saints are people who led good Christian lives and are thought to have a very close relationship to God. Only the leader of the Catholic Church, the pope, can decide to grant them sainthood. After a person dies, high-ranking Catholic officials gather proof to see if this person has lived a holy life. They also try to find proof that the person has a caused a miracle after their death—a process called beatification. But there is one exception: A martyr, someone who has died for their beliefs, can be beatified without a proven miracle.

Once these people become official saints, living Catholics look to them as role models.

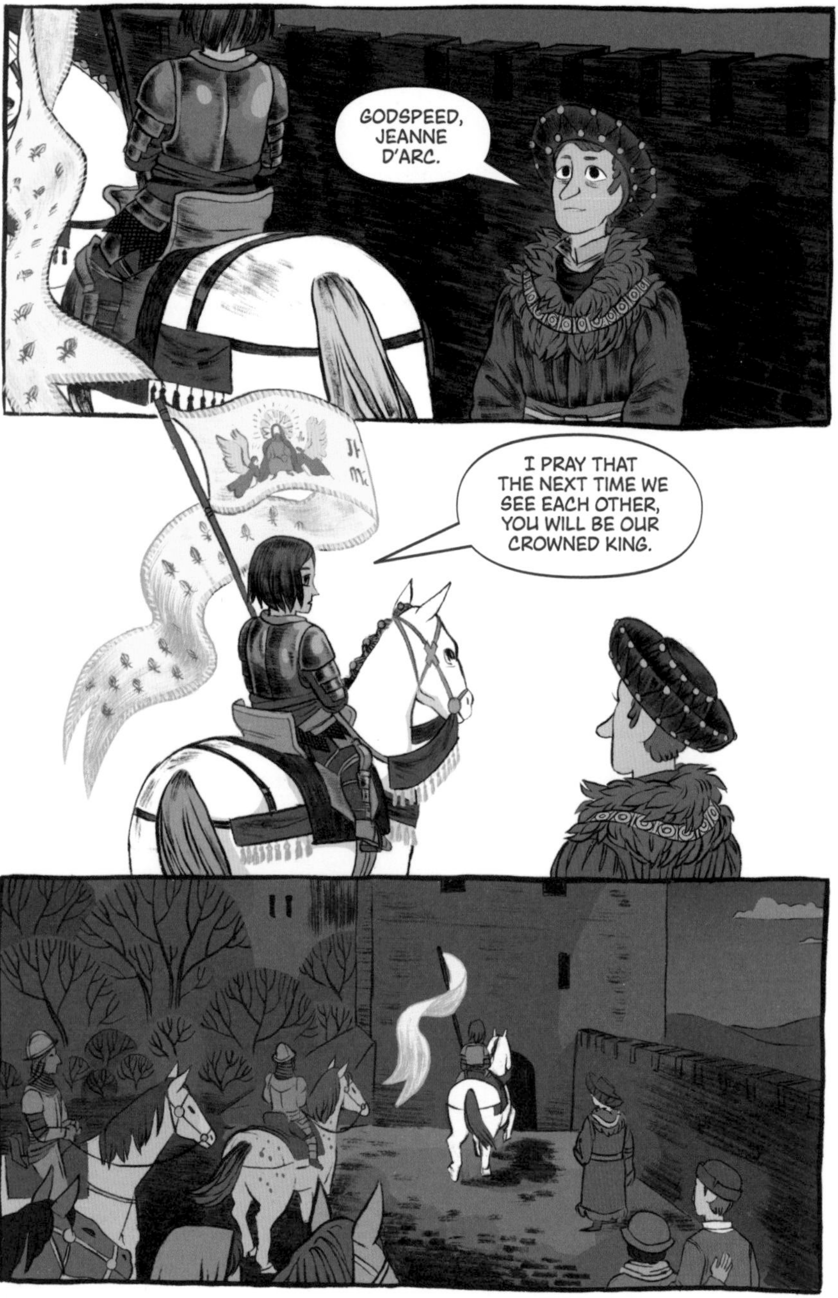
GODSPEED, JEANNE D'ARC.
I PRAY THAT THE NEXT TIME WE SEE EACH OTHER, YOU WILL BE OUR CROWNED KING.

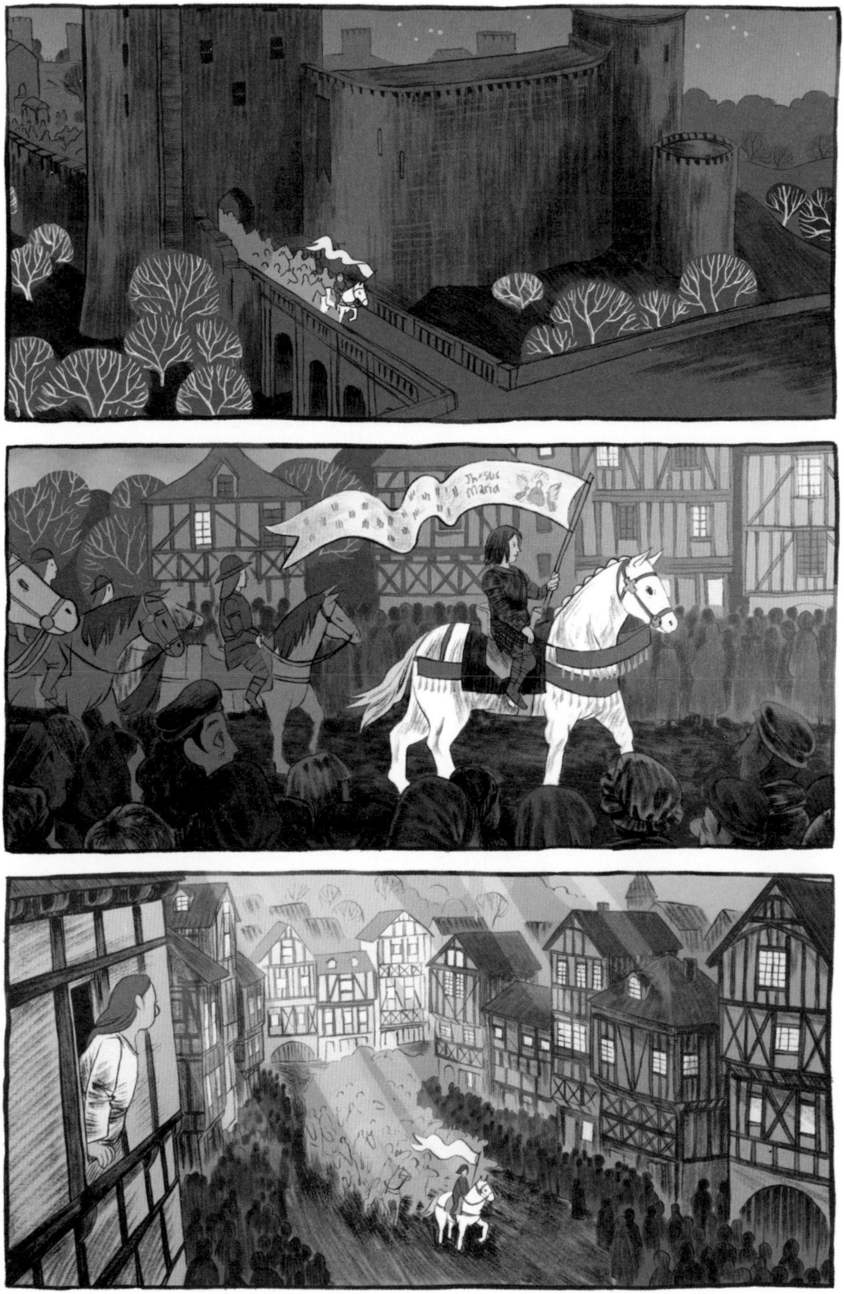
Jhesus Maria

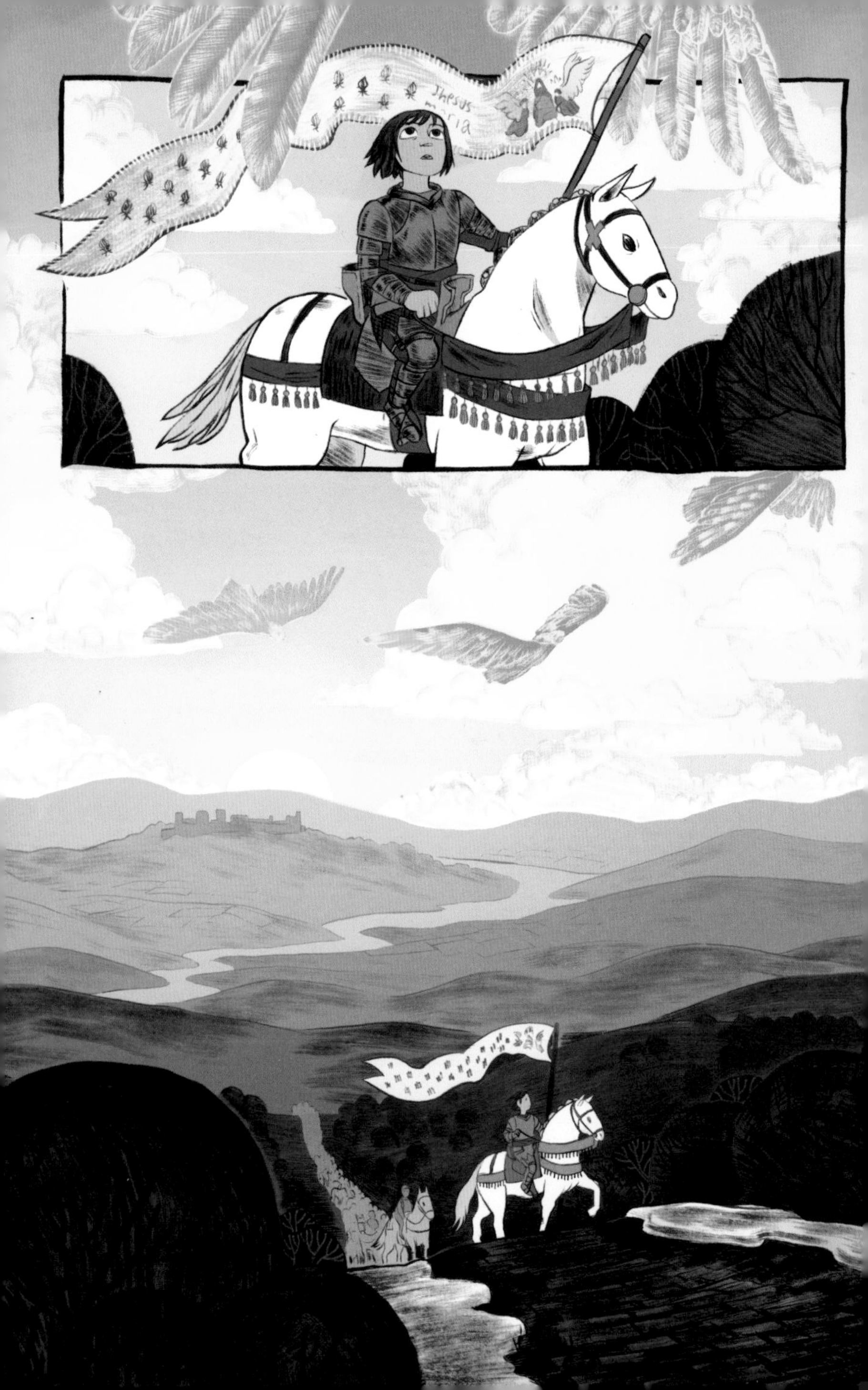
Jhesus
maria

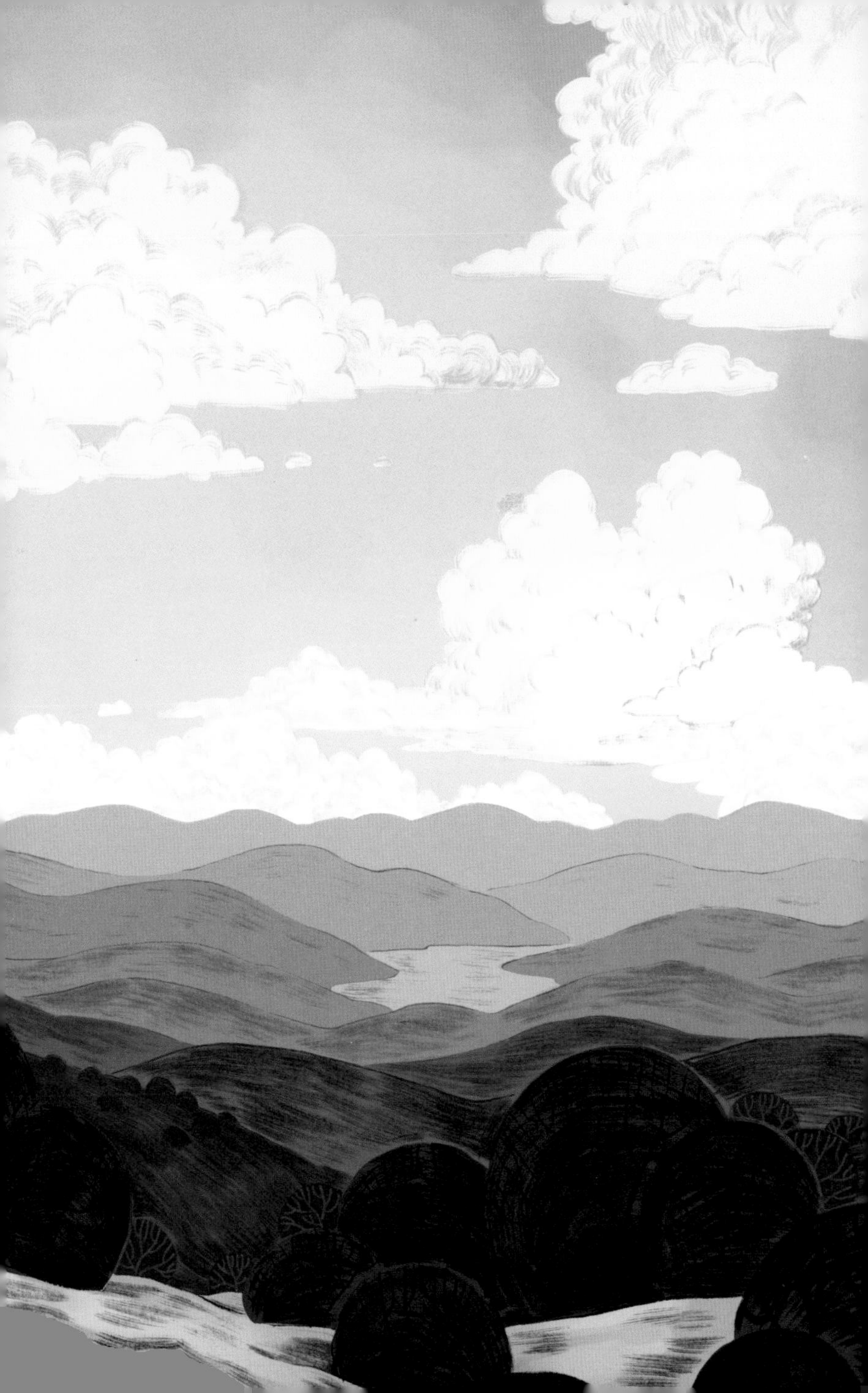

Conclusion

And so Jeanne rode to Orléans, bringing the last hope of France's freedom with her. Together with the rest of the army, she pushed English forces out of the city and saw the dauphin crowned as King Charles VII. Jeanne never used her sword to hurt another person, but she carried her banner into many battles in the Hundred Years' War and inspired France's people along the way.

England didn't like that France started winning battles again all of a sudden. The English were also Catholic and wanted to believe that God was on their side, too. So they decided what must have happened: Jeanne wasn't sent by God at all, and instead, she got her power from the Devil. It couldn't possibly be that God had abandoned them.

In May 1430, Burgundian soldiers captured Jeanne. She tried to escape their castle, but it was no use. Burgundy sold her to England, who held a trial for the heresy they thought she had committed. Jeanne explained that, with God's blessing, she wore men's clothes in order to protect herself. They still found her guilty, and Jeanne died from execution by burning in May 1431.

After Jeanne's death, Charles VII used her victories to pave the rest of the way to freedom. He gradually drove all the English invaders out of France and finally ended the war. Jeanne's mother,

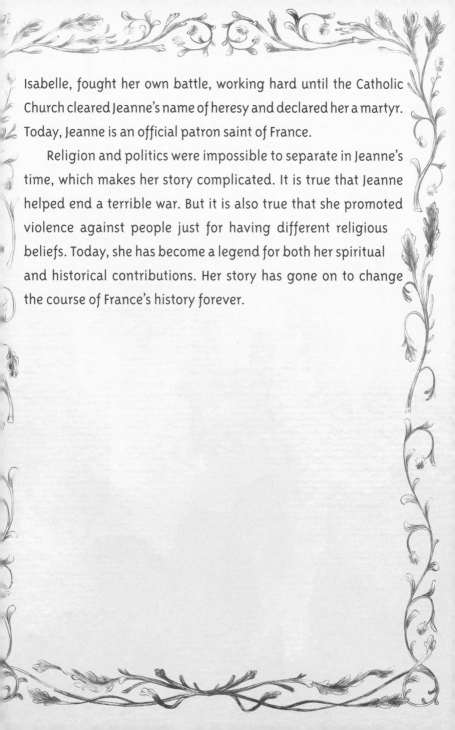

Isabelle, fought her own battle, working hard until the Catholic Church cleared Jeanne's name of heresy and declared her a martyr. Today, Jeanne is an official patron saint of France.

Religion and politics were impossible to separate in Jeanne's time, which makes her story complicated. It is true that Jeanne helped end a terrible war. But it is also true that she promoted violence against people just for having different religious beliefs. Today, she has become a legend for both her spiritual and historical contributions. Her story has gone on to change the course of France's history forever.

Timeline of Jeanne's Life

c. 1412 — Jeanne is born

1425 — Domrémy is raided, and Jeanne sees her first vision

1428 — Jeanne first visits Vaucouleurs to request Robert de Baudricourt's assistance, and he says no

— Domrémy is raided again and burned

1429 — In January, Jeanne returns to Vaucouleurs to ask for Baudricourt's help again, but this time she finds more support

— In February, the Battle of the Herrings sees France lose outside Orléans; Jeanne's prediction comes true, and Baudricourt finally agrees to help her

— In March, Jeanne meets the dauphin in Chinon

— In April, Jeanne reaches Orléans to join the fight

— In July, the dauphin is officially crowned as Charles VII, King of France

1430 — Burgundian soldiers capture Jeanne

1431 — Jeanne dies by execution after English courts find her guilty of heresy

1456 — Declared a martyr, Jeanne is cleared as innocent

1920 — The Catholic Church grants Jeanne d'Arc sainthood

Bibliography

*Books for young readers

*Brooks, Polly Schoyer. *Beyond the Myth: The Story of Joan of Arc.*
Boston: HMH Books for Young Readers, 1999.

Meissonier, Martin, dir. *The Real Joan of Arc.* Arte France Productions,
2007. Amazon Prime Video.

Pernoud, Régine, and Marie-Véronique Clin. *Joan of Arc: Her Story*.
Translated by Jeremy DuQuesnay Adams. New York: St. Martin's
Griffin, 1999.

*Pollack, Pam, and Meg Belviso. *Who Was Joan of Arc?* New York:
Penguin Workshop, 2016.

*Stanley, Diane. *Joan of Arc.* New York: HarperCollins, 2002.

*Wilkinson, Philip. *Joan of Arc: The Teenager Who Saved Her Nation.*
Washington, DC: National Geographic Children's Books, 2009.

ABOUT THE CREATORS

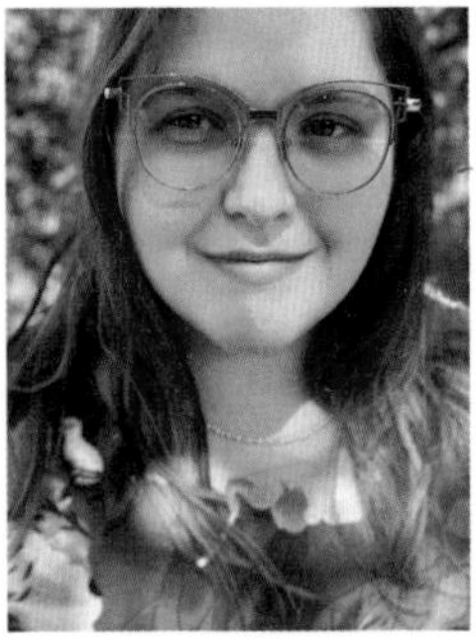

Sarah Winifred Searle

originally hails from spooky New England but currently lives in sunny Perth, Australia. She writes and draws comics for all sorts of audiences, best known for vulnerable memoir and compassionate fiction. Find her around the web: @swinsea / swinsea.com.

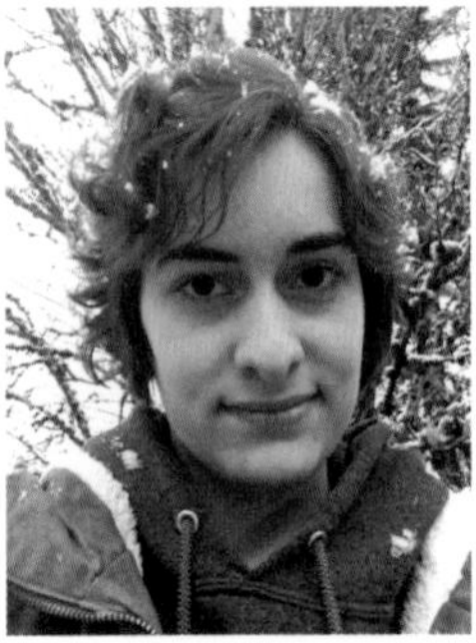

Maria Capelle Frantz

was born and raised in Fairbanks, Alaska, where she spent the first years of her life playing in the woods, making up stories, and regularly perusing the local comic shop. In 2015, she was awarded a national gold medal in the Scholastic Art and Writing Awards for her short comic "Death Wish." Her debut graphic novel, *The Chancellor and the Citadel*, was published by Iron Circus Comics in January 2019. Find her on Instagram and Twitter: @mariacfrantz.